EARLY CHILDHOOD EDUCATION SERIES

NANCY FILE & CHRISTOPHER P. BROWN, EDITORS

ADVISORY BOARD: Jie-Qi Chen, Cristina Gillanders, Jacqueline Jones,
Kristen M. Kemple, Candace R. Kuby, John Nimmo,
Amy Noelle Parks, Michelle Salazar Pérez, Andrew J. Stremmel, Valora Washington

To look for other titles in this series, visit www.tcpress.com

continued

T0355697

Early Childhood Education Series, *continued*

On Being and Well-Being in Infant/Toddler Care and Education

Life Stories From Baby Rooms

Mary Benson McMullen

Foreword by Nancy File

TEACHERS COLLEGE PRESS

TEACHERS COLLEGE | COLUMBIA UNIVERSITY
NEW YORK AND LONDON

Published by Teachers College Press,® 1234 Amsterdam Avenue, New York, NY 10027

Copyright © 2022 by Teachers College, Columbia University

Front cover images: Foot by dgrilla; hands by LaylaBird, both via iStock by Getty Images.

Library of Congress Cataloging-in-Publication Data

Names: McMullen, Mary Benson, 1958– author. | File, Nancy, writer of
     foreword.
Title: On being and well-being in infant/toddler care and education : life stories
     from baby rooms / Mary Benson McMullen ; foreword by Nancy File.
Description: New York : Teachers College Press, [2022] | Series: Early childhood
     education series | Includes bibliographical references and index.
Identifiers: LCCN 2022004421 (print) | LCCN 2022004422 (ebook) |
     ISBN 9780807766750 (hardcover) | ISBN 9780807766743 (paperback) |
     ISBN 9780807780923 (epub)
Subjects: LCSH: Early childhood education. | Early childhood educators—
     Psychology. | Infants—Care. | Toddlers—Care. | Well-being.
Classification: LCC LB1139.23 .M46 2022 (print) | LCC LB1139.23 (ebook) |
     DDC 372.21—dc23/eng/20220225
LC record available at https://lccn.loc.gov/2022004421
LC ebook record available at https://lccn.loc.gov/2022004422

ISBN 978-0-8077-6674-3 (paper)
ISBN 978-0-8077-6675-0 (hardcover)
ISBN 978-0-8077-8092-3 (ebook)

Printed on acid-free paper
Manufactured in the United States of America

To my beloved husband, Rick, for being my soulmate and best friend for the past 4 decades.

To my three babies, Brad, Mikey, and Ben, my kind, thoughtful, and funny boys, for teaching me about the joy and power of a mother's love.

And to Mikey (1985–2010), the loss of you, my sweet and cherished boy, showed me the depths and endurance of that love.

i carry your heart with me (i carry it in
my heart). i am never without you (anywhere
I go you go, my darling; and whatever is done
by only me is your doing, my darling)

E. E. Cummings (1952)

Contents

Foreword

When I started my last position, the course I was most interested in teaching was the "babies" course. It was titled Infants and Toddlers: Curriculum and Teaching. Certainly reflective of the Curriculum and Instruction department in which my program resided, but the words never sat comfortably with me. *Curriculum* as a concept needs much adjustment for the youngest children served by our field, and the traditional notions of teaching brought forward by the college students were certainly a limited perspective for the multiple sorts of interactions involved in care and education for babies. Still, there needed to be a conceptual focus for the course. At that time, we centered on the concepts of responsiveness and respect; on play and routine caregiving, as well as the everydayness of how babies live their lives.

Meanwhile, learning standards were increasingly created for use in early childhood education settings, eventually including baby rooms. Might learning standards become the conceptual focus? They may serve as indicators in the process, knowledge, and skills that we expect babies will be learning as they grow. In some instances, they reveal the dispositions we hope the babies adopt as they learn about and master their worlds. But still, there are many paths toward those indicators. Early learning standards do not seem sufficient to guide the decision-making and shape the values and attitudes of adults who care for babies. How should life in a group setting be compared to life at home for babies? Are early care and education programs an intervention in a baby's life, or an alternative space to learn and thrive while family members fulfill their own responsibilities? Where might these decisions lead the field?

This is where Mary Benson McMullen's book comes in. I've always believed that being present-oriented is key for baby rooms. It's not about who they will be in a couple, or several, years but about what everyday life is like for them right now. This is what leads a teacher, or caregiver, or "care teacher" as Mary uses, to read a book yet again (on that particular day, let alone tomorrow), to notice a new word used as they watch children at play, to realize that the ABCs, 123s, and color names will come in their time but for today there is a sponge that can be squeezed over and over as water runs down a baby's arm, or a shadow to be discovered for the first time.

The task of providing wonderful group settings for babies (and what family member doesn't want that?) requires deep reflection of a strongly developed understanding of life as a baby. What do we know about babies, and, importantly, what do we want *for* them? This is just what Mary has given us in this volume. She has provided a conceptual focus through the notions of "being" and "well-being." I must admit to completely falling for this book's title upon first hearing it! The former clarifies that decisions are based upon who babies are now, in the present. This allows babies to take their own time and path in learning about how the world works when they are new to it. The latter indicates that this life can be well-lived and meet the needs of both babies and the adults in their lives—professionals and family members. We can define what is valued and address challenges to those values being realized. The well-being concepts Mary presents in each chapter, and the big ideas she draws from them, provide a focus for how adults can decide to "be" with babies, as well as with their families.

Mary has chosen to present her ideas through story. These stories have an immediacy and intimacy that sometimes took my breath away. Innumerable decisions are made in an early care and education program, whether to shape long-term program policy or on-the-fly reactions to what is happening in the classroom. All have an impact on both the babies and adults. Perhaps the best examination of decisions is to watch what happens in action, which is what Mary's stories allow us to do. Readers who engage with her stories and reflect upon their meaning will indeed find their way to a focus for how to "be" with babies. And there are many good ways to be with babies, ways to promote the well-being concepts Mary examines while also taking into account individual styles, community settings, cultural values, and respect for differences.

In my short experience of being a grandmother, I've experienced the Zen of not being a multitasking, employed mother. The gift of fully enjoying the brilliance of this little person (which only mirrors the brilliance of all babies) has only cemented for me the importance of a conceptual focus on being and well-being, of approaching babies in regard to who they are, of making sure that they can be fully and happily well in their worlds, and that they are supported when they face difficulty as they figure out how to navigate themselves and their worlds.

Nancy File

Acknowledgments

This book is dedicated to my husband and sons, but I am also deeply indebted to my father, Marcel Benson, for always believing in me and loving me unconditionally, and my sister Sue Benson Hicks, for being my first and best teacher of how to be a good mother to babies. I thank those dear friends with whom I have shared love and loss, laughter and tears, great food and wine, and deep conversations throughout decades of my career: Marty Lash, Melissa Keller, Bobbie Partenheimer, Cary Buzzelli, Ellen Veselack, Sue Dixon, Peggy Apple, Jim Elicker, Nancy Barbour, Lara Lackey, and Julia Heimer Beebe.

I'm equally grateful for more recent friendships from others who have enriched my life and my thinking about young children, education, and so much more, including Kathy Goouch, Sacha Powell, Chris Brown, Travis Wright, Kate McCormick, Dan Castner, Dianna Huxhold, Ceci Maron Puntarelli, Mila Costa, Maria Cooper, and Carrey Siu. My thanks go also to many friends and colleagues who have influenced my beliefs about educating and advocating for young children, their families, and the professionals who work with them: Tim Dunnuck, Jasmine Zachariah, Dylan Brody, Jennifer Addleman, Samantha Sisk, Christy Smith, Linda Fields, and Amelia Galloway.

I owe much thanks to the many people who helped me on my journey as a writer including Carol Copple, Derry Koraleck, Kathy Charner, Susan Friedman, and Holly Bohart from NAEYC. Thank you for believing in me and for helping me believe I had something worth saying. I also thank Rossella Procopio, NAEYC books editor, for her superb editorial advice and motivation while writing *The Right Stuff: Play Materials for Infants, Toddlers, and Twos*, coauthored with Dylan Brody. I give a special shout-out to Lisa Wood, Sarah Alkhataff, Melissa Lee, and Nara Yun, members of my Writing Empowerment Group (WEG), for being alongside me for over a year of weekly Zoom meetings as we encouraged one another through pandemic writing projects.

And a very special thanks to Nancy File for providing the feedback, editorial advice, and encouragement that inspired me as I completed this book. Along with Nancy, I owe my sincere gratitude to Sarah Biondello, senior acquisitions editor, and all the staff at Teachers College Press, including Susan Liddicoat, Lori Tate, Caritza Berlioz, Nancy Power, and Mike Olivo who helped to make this book a reality. Many thanks to Kathy Caveney, who copyedited the manuscript. Finally, I wish to recognize the dozens, if not hundreds, of current and former students, early childhood professionals, and babies and young children and their families, too numerous to name but to whom I am indebted and will forever hold in my heart.

On Being and Well-Being in Infant/Toddler Care and Education

CHAPTER 1

Well-Being for Babies and Their Care Teachers

An Introduction

There can be no keener revelation of a society's soul than the way in which it treats its children.

—Nelson Mandela (1995, para. 1)

On any given day, there are few places I would rather be than in a baby room. With each new encounter with a group of babies and care teachers, I learn new lessons about life, love, and empathetic understanding. I have deep regard for infants and toddlers and tremendous respect for

1

those who care for and educate them. To me, babies are fascinating and charming little persons, full of life, wonder, and endless potential. I have learned much about who I am as a caring person and what I believe, just from being with them and watching them and those who engage in care with them.

I arrived at my understanding and appreciation of infants, toddlers, and those who care for and educate them through personal, educational, and professional experience. Before and during my graduate school career, I worked part- and then full-time in childcare programs. Much of that time I was an infant care teacher. This was followed by years as the director of a program for children ages birth to 5 years. Since 1993, I have been a professor of early childhood education. As part of my work, I have spent a considerable amount of time over the past 3 decades visiting infant/toddler rooms while supervising university students engaged in field experiences. As an early childhood researcher, I have conducted several studies that have brought me into baby rooms to observe the children and the adults, and to interview care teachers, administrators, and family members. And finally, my husband and I were blessed with three beautiful baby sons whom we raised into adulthood. It is my sons who were truly my best and most important teachers.

CARING FOR AND ABOUT BABIES AND THEIR CARE TEACHERS

Over the years, as I noted above, I have had the privilege to spend time with many care teachers who welcomed me into their rooms. For this, and the kindness and trust it showed, I am forever grateful. Some of those care teachers, many of whom you will encounter in this book, were truly exceptional individuals. They allowed me to share in their joys and celebrations of achievements great and small and to witness the grace with which they handled challenges and stressful moments. I have been humbled by the mindfulness I have seen them display, whether they were going about what seem to be the most mundane of tasks (e.g., cleaning tabletops, sweeping floors), or when comforting a baby who is in desperate need of having their individual and focused attention. I appreciate the many care teachers I have interviewed, formally and informally, who were able to maintain a fully professional demeanor in the baby room, while being clear-eyed and articulate about the bigger challenges they faced. Such care teachers shared with me difficulties we all understand as inherent in the childcare workplace and in the Early Childhood Care and Education (ECCE) field (e.g., issues of respect, low compensation, difficult work schedules).

From my experience, I have found that exceptionally strong infant/toddler care teachers have several attributes and dispositional traits in common. They demonstrate and maintain high levels of intellectual engagement and emotional investment in the children, their families, and the profession, even when under stressful workplace circumstances. They possess knowledge and skills specialized for working with birth- to age-3 children, but also have a broader knowledge of typical child development through the preschool years as well. They are empathetic and caring individuals, who want what is best for the infants and toddlers with whom they work, and in an intentional manner they support the families' goals related to their babies' upbringing.

Nonetheless, I am often asked, "Why care about childcare for babies?" My first response is, *because it is the right thing to do!* After taking a deep breath, and then depending upon who asked the question, I talk to them—for as long as they will listen—about various rationales that might appeal to their point-of-view or personal or professional priorities. Consider, for instance, the following information as ways we can justify the importance of examining and understanding childcare for children birth- to 3-years:

- *Supply and Demand*—In the United States and across the world, access to affordable childcare is what a UNICEF report (Samman & Lombardi, 2019) described as a "global crisis," with the greatest unmet need being for professional (nonfamilial) infant and toddler care (Workman & Jessen-Howard, 2018). This need has occurred largely because of rising family income and the economic realities of national economies dependent on increased workforce participation. Thus mothers and fathers, aunties and uncles, grandparents, and neighbors living nearby who may have taken care of babies in the past are now more likely to be engaged in full- or part-time work and therefore unavailable (Business Research Company, 2019).
- *Appropriate Practices with Infants and Toddlers*—The care and education of children under the age of 3 remains the least studied developmental period within the field of ECCE, resulting in an incomplete understanding of the best or most appropriate curriculum and pedagogy for this age group (Cooper et al., 2021; Horm et al., 2012; Zero to Three, 2008, 2017). This is despite ever increasing understanding of the importance of the first three years, arising from the following:
  - » Neurobiological (brain) research and decades of educational and psychological research showing that the most rapid and critical period of physical, cognitive, language, and social and emotional growth and development occurs in the first three years (Bust & Pedro, 2020; Goldstein et al., 2007; Institute of Medicine and

National Research Council, 2012; McMullen, 2013; Raikes & Edwards, 2009; UNICEF, 2017)

  » Consistent findings that the quality of infant/toddler childcare matters and has long-lasting impact (Bratsch-Hines et al., 2020; Start Early, 2020)

- *Social Equity*—An in-depth understanding of practices in infant/toddler childcare is necessary for policymakers and community leaders concerned with meeting the demand for safe, affordable, quality childcare for *all* families with babies who need it, regardless of socioeconomic status or geographic location (CLASP, 2015; Rice et al., 2019; Workman & Jessen-Howard 2018; Keating et al., 2019). Although all infants, toddlers, and young children benefit from quality childcare experiences, this is especially true for children experiencing poverty and those who come from low-resourced households and communities (Laurin et al., 2015; Loeb et al., 2004; McCartney et al., 2007; Owen et al., 2008) and for children with special needs (Novoa, 2020).

- *Workforce Development*—There is a need to challenge discourses that minimize the importance of the care and education of infants and toddlers that have resulted in the marginalization of its workforce, lower expectations for the qualifications of those who work in this specialized field, and a lack of adequate compensation in terms of wages and other benefits. Such undervaluing is discouraging to those who work in the field and can have profound impact on the recruitment and the retention of highly qualified care teachers (Austin, 2018). In addition, it affects care teachers' capacity to care, fully and mindfully, for the babies and families with whom they work (Cumming, 2017; Jeon et al., 2018; Kwon et al., 2020; McMullen et al., 2020; McMullen & McCormick, 2016).

I wrote this book for those of you who are currently ECCE professionals or are students preparing for careers working with infants and toddlers (babies) and their families. I want to honor and celebrate babies who spend much of their daily lives in childcare and to elevate the adults who dedicate themselves to their care and education. In this book I have rendered portraits of care and education in the form of short stories that I call "life stories" created from my own day-to-day lived experiences within the walls and outdoor play spaces of baby rooms.

My primary goals in writing this book were threefold. First, I present the life stories to provoke birth-to-3 professionals and students to reflect upon their own beliefs about how very young children grow, develop, and learn, and to thoughtfully consider the caring behaviors in which they engage when they are with them. Second, I intended for the practices and scenarios portrayed to act as prompts for critical dialogue among groups of colleagues or classmates who read the book together. Third, I wrote this book as a call to action—a call to care or to care more profoundly about how babies and care teachers spend their days together in the baby rooms of childcare settings.

EXPLANATION OF THE TERMS IN THIS BOOK

To help orient you to the terminology in this book, I offer a list of words and phrases as I will use them from this point forward. My choices of certain terms may provoke a response and perhaps disagreement from some readers; if so, I invite you to use it as a point for discussion and debate with your professional colleagues or fellow students.

Administrator(s): *The adults who are responsible for the overall functioning of a program, such as directors, principals, owners, managers, and supervisors.* I chose the term *administrator* because it includes all these roles, and perhaps others, that indicate the person has some degree of control, power, decision-making authority, and/or responsibility for the overall childcare programs featured in the life stories in this book. In doing so, I also recognize that some leadership styles result in administrators who share power with others in a program.

Baby/Babies: *Infants and toddlers, sometimes referred to as "very young children," those from birth to about a child's second birthday, the end of what UNICEF and the American Academy of Pediatrics refer to as the first 1,000 days* (Cusick & Georgieff, 2013; 1,000 Days, 2016; Schwarzenberg & Georgieff, n.d.). For this age group, I prefer the terms *baby* and *babies* to remind myself and others that these children are very young and that they are entirely different from preschoolers (3- to 5-year-olds) in how they look, think, and act, and in how they understand their emotions and their place in the world. Babyhood is a unique period of development that should be recognized and celebrated on its own apart from other periods of early childhood. All babies in the life stories in this book are under 18 months of age.

Baby Room(s): *A childcare room or rooms purposefully set up for the care and education of babies.* I prefer this term to that of *classrooms* when speaking of or about childcare spaces for babies. My preference for this term comes from years spent doing research with international colleagues and observations within other countries in which *classroom* is rarely if ever used to describe rooms and settings for very young children. I was told emphatically by one of these colleagues, that the idea of classrooms for babies is an absurd notion that conjures up images of traditional education spaces with teachers standing in front of babies seated at desks.

Care Teachers(s): *The adults in the baby rooms discussed in this book who are the employees responsible for the day-to-day direct care and education of groups of babies and their families in childcare settings.* Using the term *care teacher* rather than *teacher* is not in any way meant to diminish the professionalism of these individuals. On the contrary, I use this term to reclaim and elevate the critical aspect of care in their professional role, one I find too often marginalized in the field of Early Childhood *Care* and Education. I also avoid using the term *caregiver* in recognition that for some of us, this term is problematic because it implies that caring is a one-way proposition. In other words, it suggests there is one person holding the power to "give" care, failing to capture the relational aspects of caring. Thus, in using the term *care teacher*, I intend to foreground the caring, relational aspects of this role. Although I recognize that some emphasize the dualism of care and education using the term *educare* and associated terms *educarer* and *educaring*, which are popular among those following the RIE (Resources for Infant Educarers) Approach (RIE, n.d.), I find that term cumbersome. My use of care teacher is also influenced by some of the exceptional infant/toddler professionals I have worked with who, when given the choice, embraced the title of care teacher. One of them described the reason she takes pride in a job title that includes "care" by saying: "You cannot care without educating, but you can educate without care. They must both be present." Finally, my adoption of the term *care teacher* was inspired by its use by a former doctoral student of mine, Nara Yun, who uses this term in her research and when describing her role working with toddlers.

Childcare Program: *The setting in which care and education is provided to groups of children.* For this book, the childcare programs described are center-based programs with baby rooms for children under the age of 2. They are all affiliated with major universities and located on college campuses.

Continuity of Care: *The practice of keeping groups of children together with their care teachers over an extended period, often 2 to 3 years* (Garrity et al., 2015; Horm et al., 2018; McMullen, 2018; McMullen et al., 2015). Of the four baby rooms featured in this book, three of them practiced continuity of care. Two of the rooms used a "looping" model in which children begin as young infants and stay with their care teachers until the summer after their third birthday (Hegde & Cassidy, 2004), whereas the third room achieved continuity through "multiage grouping" that included children from 6-weeks of age to 2 years of age (Anderson, 2018). Continuity of care differs from the more traditional model in which children are moved to the next room with new care teachers each year sometime during the summer; or there is what I call the "revolving door" practice in which children are constantly coming and going through the year based upon achievement of some milestone (e.g., reaching a birthday, becoming mobile, being toilet trained) (McMullen, 2017).

Family/Families: *The related or non-related adults and children that comprise babies' home lives.* Throughout the book, I rarely use the term *parent* because not all babies are raised by parents; I prefer the broader terms *family* and *families.* At times that I do use *mother* or *father* in the text, it is because it is a direct reference to a character featured in a story who identifies themselves as such.

Family-Centered or Whole-Family Care: *Incorporation of family members into the care team, along with the professional care teachers, as important partners in the setting of goals and making decisions about the child's care.* I use this term to indicate that this is something beyond just including or involving the family but rather working in true partnership with them (Dunst et al., 2019; McMullen, 2013; Ziviani et al., 2011).

Key (or Primary) Person Care: *The practice widely recommended in infant/toddler care that refers to the assignment of each of the care teachers in a baby room to a small group of children and their families to provide particular, but not exclusive, focus, in terms of major care responsibilities, record keeping, and communication with family members* (Bernhardt, 2000; Ebbeck et al., 2015; Elfer 2013; Zero to Three, 2010). The baby rooms featured in this book differed in whether they formally assigned key persons, with two rooms assigning them, one room appointing them only for the initial few weeks of enrollment, and the fourth room having no familiarity with the concept.

Life Stories: *Accounts of the events that happen to someone in their life.* In this book I chronicle some of my own lived experiences, rendering them as life stories of time spent in baby rooms over the past 12 years or so. I focus these stories on events in the lives of the adults and babies who worked and played in these settings.

Lived Experiences: Refers to the meanings made by individuals of the events, relationships, and environments they encounter as perceived cognitively and emotionally. This perspective on lived experiences comes from my reading of Vygtosky's concept of *perezhivanie,* which he used to explain how it is through thinking + feeling that we come to make sense of encounters and events in our lives (Brennan, 2014; Clarà, 2016; Fleer et al., 2017; McMullen et al., 2020; Vygotsky, 1934/1987). In part, this view helps explain why two people who seem to encounter the same thing, even at the same moment, may experience it very differently.

Well-Being: *A general state of being and feeling well in terms of physical and psychological health and safety, emotional stability and soundness, and overall satisfaction in activities and relationships* (McMullen et al., 2016, p. 262). The life stories in this book are organized around the following elements of well-being for babies and adults in baby rooms: comfort and security; belonging, respect, and communication; engagement and contribution; and efficacy and agency (McMullen et al., 2020). Later in this chapter, each of these elements of well-being is described in some detail as they frame the stories presented in Chapters 2 through 5.

CURATED LIFE STORIES

For many of us, when we encounter the words *curate, curating,* and *curators*, what comes to mind are museums and works of art. But according to the online *MacMillan Dictionary* the verb, *to curate,* is not reserved for the arts; rather, it means, "to select items from among a large number of possibilities for other people to consume or enjoy." The term has become popular across multiple domains beyond the arts, being used by restaurant owners, clothing boutiques, book collectors, and many more (Williams, 2009). It has also been adopted by educators (Cherrstrom & Boden, 2020), including early childhood educators (Eriksson, 2018; McMullen & Brody, 2021) who speak of themselves as curators of educational resources, spaces, and curriculum practices.

For this book, I present myself to you as a curator of lived experiences in baby rooms that I have purposefully selected from my own collection of life stories. Like a curator of a museum exhibit, I made deliberate choices about which life stories to share and how to present—or display—them. Also like a curator of art works, while I provide background and context for these curated pieces, I provide interpretation only in the form of short reflections of key ideas I identify within the scenes portrayed. Just as we all create our own meanings when we see a painting on a wall or watch a dancer on a stage, I urge you to let these life stories speak to you— cognitively and emotionally—on a personal level. Consider alternative and more personally relevant meanings and co-construct new ways to think

about them in dialogue with one another. The usefulness of this is supported by Breault (2009), who spoke of the importance of story in the professional development of teachers, arguing that the role of the storyteller is to
"reveal meaning without defining it" (p. 400). To this end, I provide questions and prompts to stimulate thinking at the end of each of my personal
reflections of the stories.

The telling of the life stories in this book represents a culmination of
personal reflections and data from my research involving infants and toddlers in four different baby rooms on university campuses across the mid-
western United States over a period of about twelve years. This research
and the resulting publications involved five main areas of related work
that directly involved baby rooms and focused on the following:

- Prosocial behaviors in infant/toddler rooms (McMullen et al.,
  2009)
- Relationship-based infant/toddler practices (McMullen & Apple,
  2012; McMullen & Dixon, 2009)
- Continuity of care for infants, toddlers, and their families
  (McMullen, 2017, 2018; McMullen et al., 2016)
- Differing missions of infant care on university campuses
  (McMullen & Lash, 2012)
- Pedagogies of care for 1-year-olds across four cultures (Cooper
  et al., 2022; Costa & McMullen, 2020)

I primarily used ethnographic case-study methods, taking a phenomenological approach (Patterson, 2018; Pitard, 2019). The "phenomenon" in
common across these bodies of work is "daily life in baby rooms" in
which I explored the lived experiences of babies, care teachers, administrators, and families as they spent their days together interacting with
environments, forming and nurturing relationships, and engaging in various activities and practices.

The Power of Stories

"Stories have the power to direct and change our lives."

—Nel Noddings (1991, p. 157)

Cultural anthropologists speak of stories and storytelling as being at the
heart of who we are as human beings, something that sets us apart from
other animals (Bruner, 1984). The passing on of stories from one genera-
tion to another is a phenomenon found across all cultures. "Human beings have lived out and told stories about the living for as long as we could
talk. And then we have talked about the stories we tell for almost as long"

(Clandinin & Rosiek, 2007, p. 35). It is through our own and others' stories that we make sense of the world around us and our place within it, and that we share that understanding with others. As Polkinghorne (1988) stated, it is through stories that "human experiences are made meaningful" (p. 1). Furthermore, as concluded in a brain research study published by the University of Southern California (2017), the stories of others have "a widespread effect on triggering better self-awareness and empathy for others." (para. 3).

Stories do more than convey the lore, traditions, and history of human experience and who we are within it (Rose, 2011), they also inspire and teach and lead individuals forward (Boris, 2017; Renken, 2020; Swap et al., 2015). According to Boris, what makes stories and storytelling so important and effective in learning is: "For starters, storytelling forges connections among people, and between people and ideas (para. 1) . . . They build familiarity and trust and allow the listener to enter the story where they are, making them more open to learning" (para. 3). It is for these reasons that storytelling is often used in teacher education and professional development (Breault, 2009; Carter, 1993). As Noddings and Witherell (1991) said, stories about educators, "provide us with a picture of real people, in real situations, struggling with real problems" (p. 280).

With the life stories that I curated for this book, I tried to do as Boris (2017) suggested and include different points of entry through which practitioners could make "connections," and I have attempted to be transparent and honest in order to create a sense of "familiarity and trust" with the reader. I hope those who see parts of themselves in the stories may come to understand themselves and others who engage in this work more deeply and more compassionately. And although the life stories were selected to create feelings of intimacy in which care teachers and students may be able to connect to and empathize with the characters or situations, I tried to provide readers the opportunity to remain at a comfortable distance.

How you connect with and make meaning of what you read in this book brings me back to an earlier discussion. Neuroscience speaks to the power of stories being the strong connection they make with the parts of the brain that process empathy and emotional engagement with language and understanding. You may recall, I described this as the phenomenon of *perezhivanie*, as I have interpreted it from Vygotsky's work (i.e., lived experience = cognition + emotion). Zak (2013) described how these brain processes allow for "narrative transportation" into the world and experiences of characters featured in stories. Furthermore, Zak claimed stories motivate us, "to look inside ourselves and make changes to become better people" (para. 28), which speaks to the value of stories for personal growth and learning. Our brains naturally seek to relate stories to our own experiences (Widrich, 2012), making stories, according to Rosen (2018), an important tool for the professional development of care teachers.

Taking a Goodness Perspective

As I explained earlier, the life stories in this book represent my personal experiences in baby rooms in which I documented and studied the lived experiences of babies and care teachers, administrators, and families within those settings. Some of the life stories in Chapters 2 through 5 are faithful retellings of events as they occurred, portrayed as accurately as I could reconstruct them from my memories, interview transcripts, photographs, and field journals. Other life stories are composites drawn from two or more incidents that were similar. I created composites primarily to highlight certain phenomena common across different baby rooms, or events that were not just one instance, but that occurred consistently, over time. Other times I use composites to describe behaviors that may have troubled me in some way, and I wish to protect the identity of persons or places so as not to embarrass or cause hurt feelings.

In all cases, even in places where my tone is critical, I try not to sound overly harsh or judgmental. You can decide for yourself how well I achieved this sometimes-difficult goal! My intention while rendering these life stories was to take a "goodness" perspective in their presentation, as suggested by Lawrence-Lightfoot (2005) and Lawrence-Lightfoot and Davis (1997). This point of view recognizes that all the adults portrayed in the stories were well-intentioned and doing what they believed to be best. I admit to moments of uncertainty as I attempted to apply this goodness perspective when I recount certain situations or environments that particularly challenged my own beliefs and sensibilities. However, I tried to be as charitable as possible to the characters in the portrayals, giving them the benefit of the doubt by assuming they all wanted what was "best" for the babies; I urge you to try to do the same. Please critique constructively and kindly, taking care to consider the circumstances and constraints under which various characters may be working (i.e., in terms of environment and infrastructure, level of knowledge and expertise, policies, administrative support, and so on).

A WELL-BEING FRAMEWORK

Increasingly, attention is being paid by researchers, advocates, and professionals about issues that impact ECCE professionals and the work that they do, beyond just looking at their qualifications, years of service, and beliefs about young children (Jeon et al., 2018; McCormick et al., 2021; Raghavan & Alexandrova, 2015; Slot, 2018). Major national efforts to address the well-being of ECCE professionals directly, such as the Happy Teacher Project (Kwon et al., 2021) and Promoting Staff Well-Being initiated by Head Start's Early Childhood Learning and Knowledge Center (Head Start/ECLKC, 2020), testify to this.

Well-being may be a familiar term for most people, and in general we all think of it as referring to something positive. The term is ubiquitous, found nearly everywhere and attached to various disciplines and constructs (e.g., economic well-being, physical or emotional health and well-being, spiritual well-being), but rarely is *well-being* defined on its own. According to Ben-Arieh and his colleagues (2014), who research children's well-being across the world:

> Definitions of well-being emphasize a desirable state of being happy, healthy, or prosperous; that is, well-being refers to both subjective feelings and experiences as well as to living conditions. Well-being is also related to the fulfillment of desires, to the balance of pleasure and pain, and to opportunities for development and self-fulfillment. (p. 1)

Seligman (2011) furthered our understanding of well-being, calling it a construct that has five elements, including positive emotion, engagement, positive relationships, meaning, and achievement. He went on to say, "No one element defines well-being, but each contributes to it" (p. 24).

I have framed the "story chapters" of this book (Chapters 2–5) around elements that my research team and I have identified as contributing to the well-being of the very young children and adults in baby rooms. As defined in the list above, well-being in this context addresses how "well" an individual, whether a baby or a grown-up, both *is* and *feels* physically, emotionally, and psychologically. In some of our past publications, my research associates and I outlined 9 Senses of Well-Being as elements that contribute to the lived experience of wellness in young children (McMullen et al., 2016) and in the professionals who engage with them in childcare (McCormick & McMullen, 2019; McCormick et al., 2021; McMullen & McCormick, 2016; McMullen, McCormick, & Lee, 2018).

Seeing Through a Well-Being Lens

What does it mean to take a well-being perspective as it concerns both babies and adult professionals in childcare? Seeing babies through a well-being lens requires me to concentrate most of my attention on who they are and what happens to them in the here and now, in the moment

(Matthews, 1998; McMullen et al., 2016), rather than focusing on some distant time in the future. Qvortrup (2009) spoke of this as treating children as "human beings" rather than just "human becomings," cautioning that the latter leads to a singular focus on what he called, "outcome thinking" (p. 632). Children's well-being researchers Raghavan and Alexandrova (2015) supported the importance of the here and now: "A good childhood is valuable not only because it leads to successful adulthood, but also for its own sake" (p. 897).

I believe babies, our youngest citizens, have rights, and implicit in this view is that they have the right to live, each and every day, fully, safely, and happily. My focus on the present—babies as human *beings*—does not, however, exclude concern for babies' futures—who they may become. Quite the opposite; I believe that focusing on the present is the only way to optimize a healthy future. In other words, I firmly believe a focus on individual babies, in the moment, rather than obsessing over readiness for some distant future, is foundational to optimizing healthy overall development, learning, and well-being as babies grow. It is our job as care teachers and members of society-at-large, therefore, to ensure that babies in baby rooms receive the type of care and education necessary to ensure these rights every single day, and to provide the environments, experiences, and relationships that will lead each of them into a healthy future.

The well-being perspective I take for the care teachers in baby rooms is similarly focused on the "now" in terms of how the wellness of these adults impacts their perceptions of and ability to function within their daily workplace realities. As my colleagues and I expressed it in an earlier publication:

> Anyone who has flown has heard a flight attendant say some version of this caution: *In case it becomes necessary to use oxygen masks, and you are traveling with a small child, put on your own mask first, and then put on your child's.* Think about that for a moment. As parents or care teachers, our natural instinct in a crisis is to immediately protect the children we are with. But losing oxygen, even briefly, can impact our physical responses and ability to think clearly. If we cannot function at full capacity, we actually put those in our care at higher risk! We must be at our best to respond fully and appropriately to the needs of those around us. (McMullen et al., 2018, p. 16)

Professional well-being affects care teachers' capacity to care mindfully, appropriately, and sensitively for the babies and families with whom they work (Cumming, 2017; Jeon et al., 2018; Kwon et al., 2019). Our research team saw the idea of "capacity to care" as building on inferences from Edward Tronick's (2007) "still face experiment."

Lack of well-being increases ECCE professionals' thoughts of leaving their current positions as well as thoughts of leaving the field of ECCE, increasing the risk of turnover (Kwon et al., 2020; McCormick et al., 2021; McMullen et al., 2020). Turnover is a problem because it disrupts the continuity of care by breaking important relational bonds between and among care teachers, babies and families, and coworkers. Careful consideration of policies and practices that promote well-being in ECCE professionals can help them thrive, feel fulfilled, and focus more fully on their work.

The Elements of Well-Being

As noted above, identification of elements that contribute to well-being in childcare emerged from years of study in which my research team and I deconstructed what it takes for individuals in these settings to be and feel well. We characterized nine distinct ways that individuals make sense of well-being cognitively and emotionally as unique to each child's or adult's lived experience within the childcare environment. In conceptualizing well-being, we were inspired by Maslow's (1943) Hierarchy of Needs. We reimagined Maslow's well-known pyramid model to stress our new understanding that all elements of the hierarchy were important to overall wellness. Specifically, rather than the additive, stepwise progression defined in Maslow's model, beginning with physiological and safety needs and ending at the pinnacle with self-actualization, we created a holistic circular model. This configuration suggests all elements are important to being and feeling well overall.

Figure 1.1 shows the mapping of the nine senses of well-being onto the levels of needs and motivations of Maslow's hierarchical model. In addition, our new circular image shows how the nine senses of well-being interact together holistically within the physical environment, the

Figure 1.1. Relationship of Maslow's Hierarchy of Needs to McMullen's Holistic Model of Well-Being in Baby Rooms

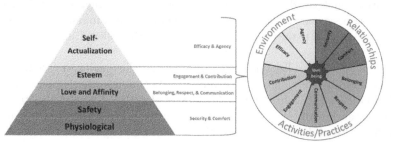

relationships between and among adults and children, and the various pedagogical practices of the adults and the activities and experiences of the children.

Well-Being in the Life Stories

The senses of well-being serve as the common thread woven through the short life stories told in the next four chapters. The focus on well-being provides a lens for initial interpretation, deliberation, and conversations about the stories. Chapters 2 through 5 begin with a detailed description of the particular senses of well-being that are the focus for the chapter. This is followed by the telling of three stories related to those senses of well-being, each starting with a preamble to provide context. After each story, I reflect upon one or more "big ideas" that emerged to me as central to understanding the message of the story as I experienced it. I then provide prompts or questions for readers in an invitation for further reflection and discussion. A brief outline of the Senses of Well-Being and Big Ideas in each chapter is as follows:

- Chapter 2
    » Senses of Well-Being: Comfort and Security
    » Big Ideas: family-centered, whole-family care; sensitively responsive care; and primary (key person) caregiving.
- Chapter 3
    » Senses of Well-Being: Belonging, Respect, and Communication
    » Big Ideas: the right to be heard and understood; temperament and goodness of fit; and observational learning and unintended messages.
- Chapter 4
    » Senses of Well-Being: Engagement and Contribution
    » Big Ideas: empathy and prosocial behaviors of babies; respecting work and play in baby rooms; and developmentally appropriate play in baby rooms.
- Chapter 5
    » Senses of Well-Being: Efficacy and Agency
    » Big Ideas: empowering babies through child-centered scaffolding; shared power in decision-making; the power of long-term relationships.

The reflections that follow each story are from my own perspective. But as I said earlier, the real power in a story is that it can convey different meanings to different people. I encourage you to find your own meanings based upon your own lived experiences and to share those with others.

Each story has an integrity of its own and thus can be considered individually or as grouped with the others in the chapter. I encourage you to compare stories across chapters using themes that emerge. You may find new meanings in the stories by rearranging the order in which I have chosen to present them by using themes more personally or professionally meaningful to you. For instance, some of you may want to look at stories about children separately from those about professionals or focus on stories that involve family members or just one program. Some may wish to examine the stories with a critical lens, looking at issues of power and privilege, or inequities and apparent biases. In the end, I hope you will conclude, as I did, that all of the senses of well-being are important, that we must put all of the pieces together to create a coherent, holistic understanding of the well-being of babies, their families, and the professionals who care for and educate them in our baby rooms. (See Figure 1.2.)

In the final chapter, Closing Thoughts, I reflect upon what the journey of sharing the stories and writing this book has meant to me personally. I present my vision of care and education for the world's babies as something that is "In Our Hands," our responsibility both as ECCE professionals and as human beings who care about the healthy growth, development, and well-being of *all* babies. I articulate this as a call to care for all babies and families, care teachers, and administrators, those now and in the future, who spend their days in baby rooms. I call on researchers to devote more effort to examining what happens within these important spaces, and teacher educators to consider how best to prepare and provide ongoing support for adults to work effectively within them. Finally, I call on advocates to encourage continual improvement of systems to optimally support babies and their families.

Figure 1.2. Putting All of the Pieces Together

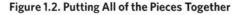

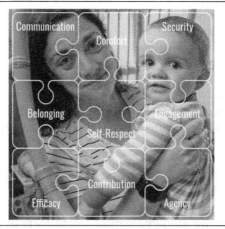

GARDENS FOR BABIES: THE ENVIRONMENT SPEAKS

In planning this book, I initially felt adrift in the sea of data collected from various baby-room studies. I searched for a way to capture the unique look and feel of each of four baby rooms that have been a focus of my research over the years. I wanted something that would allow me to feature the strengths of each setting, while being transparent and realistic when describing each space's challenges. In pondering this, I began to envision the baby rooms as places in which babies grew and thrived by being nurtured, and noted how I had witnessed this occur sometimes more and sometimes less effectively in the different spaces. Stealing unashamedly from Friedrich Froebel's (1782–1852) "kindergarten" (garden for children), I decided to use the metaphor of "growing places" to sort out my own understanding of the four rooms and as a way to try to make the spaces come alive for readers. In addition to using garden metaphors for the four different baby rooms, I use pseudonyms for the names of the care teachers, family members, and children portrayed in these spaces.

In the following sections, I set the scenes for the life stories by creating a sense of the physical nature and atmosphere of the baby rooms using the metaphors of a meditation garden, wildflower meadow, botanical garden, and a laboratory greenhouse. I use these metaphors to help distinguish the physical environments and emotional climates of the rooms and to provide context for the stories as they are read and discussed. I hope you will find this helpful as you picture the various characters and events in the stories. I begin by providing a depiction of each type of garden including its aesthetic qualities (e.g., beauty, order or disorder, emotions evoked) ending with a statement of potential challenges presented in each. This is followed by a brief word sketch of each room as it relates to the metaphor. Characterizing these life stories in this way adds another layer for consideration as you deliberate on the stories and engage in dialogue with colleagues.

Author, early childhood scholar, and former kindergarten teacher, Bill Ayers, once told my students, when visiting as a guest speaker, "The environment speaks!" He went on to tell a story about taking his kindergarteners on a field trip to an airport (back when we could do such things!). Upon encountering a long, wide, and nearly empty hallway, and despite telling the children to walk, without exception, they took off running at full tilt. He asked, "What had the environment said to them?" At this point, he raised his voice in emphasis. "THE ENVIRONMENT SAID, RUN!"

What does your environment say? As you read about the baby rooms, consider the following:

- What does our garden for babies look like?
- How do you and others feel when they are in it?

- How does your garden grow as you adapt to changing needs?
- Do you tend your garden carefully, mindfully?
- What does your environment *say* when one encounters it the first time?
- Does it support the overall physical, psychological, and emotional well-being of all within it—adults and children?

Meditation Garden—Peaceful and Respectful

A meditation garden, an example of which is shown in Figure 1.3, is designed to evoke a calming of spirit and mind, and to elicit peaceful thoughts and feelings in those who visit. It is filled with an abundance of beautiful things to see, hear, and smell, although not so much as to overwhelm the senses. While it is a natural environment, it is intentionally designed with structures, plants, and flowers that are cultivated to create a peaceful atmosphere, one that encourages mindfulness, contemplation, and reverence. And though carefully shaped and tended, it still feels natural and open to new possibilities. This environment essentially says, "This is a quiet space." Challenge: Such a space is not for everyone because for some, such a quiet space seems to have a lack opportunity for spontaneity and excitement and may foster boredom.

Figure 1.3. A Meditation Garden

The Meditation Garden Baby Room was a pleasant and peaceful space for the eight babies, two co-lead care teachers, and one aide to spend their days. It was open and airy, and well-ventilated with plenty of natural light. The ambience was warm and inviting with natural colors and woods used throughout. Fabric mobiles and swaths of pastel-colored translucent cloth hung from the ceiling, softening the environment that could otherwise feel institutional. Those arriving at the door of this room were asked by a politely worded sign to remove their shoes. They were provided slippers or allowed to walk in their stocking feet when they entered. And although there was a low hum of activity that could be heard in this space, it was generally quiet. Rarely would one feel a sense of urgency in the Meditation Garden Baby Room.

Although she is a co-lead care teacher in the room with another professional and an aide, Lily Grace set the tone in the room, her very nature seeming to define the space physically and emotionally. She arrived long before others in the morning, as she "set the table" for the children, speaking to others about what a "blessing and privilege" it was to be a part of their lives. She was mesmerizing to watch as she joyfully went about the business of preparing the room. It was easy to become caught up in the smooth rhythm and flow of the music of life in this room—both literal and figurative—as Lily Grace hummed and sang softly to herself and the babies. The words that come to mind for me from being in this space were *peaceful* and *respectful,* because this was a place where deep honor and reverence were shown to babies and families.

Wildflower Meadow—Joyful and Spontaneous

A walk through a wildflower meadow, like the one shown in Figure 1.4, provides a feast for the senses, greeting visitors with its riot of colors, smells, sounds, tactile experiences, and even, potentially, tastes. Senses are stimulated by splashes of color from a vast diversity of untamed flowers and the variety of smells they emit, butterflies and song-birds fill the air with sound, fresh air brushes cheeks and sunshine warms the skin, wild berries and sprigs from edible plants delight the taste buds. But this environment also has stinging bees and nettles, prickly bushes and thorny shrubs, and the occasional rock to stumble on or pebble to get stuck in one's shoe. This environment essentially says, "This is a fun, exciting, and stimulating space." Challenge: This environment may not be for everyone, however, because what happens is often unpredictable and may provide more stimulation than some find comfortable.

The Wildflower Meadow Baby Room was a very small room, but it was wide open in terms of possibilities for excitement and stimulation.

Figure 1.4. A Wildflower Meadow

The emotional climate was one of friendliness and feelings of being cared for happening simultaneously within the experience of boisterous, good-humored fun and a near constant anticipation of excitement. There was much in the room to delight the senses and to keep busy babies occupied, although because of its small size, the room could feel overly loud, bright, and a bit crowded at times. Sometimes unpleasant odors lingered from the kitchen and diaper area, both open to the main playroom. Big bright windows filled the room with natural light and there was always plenty for the babies to view on the sidewalk just outside—busy people passing, the lawn being mowed, packages being delivered, and their "friend" Doug, who delivered meals.

The two co-lead care teachers, Vivian and Lucy, filled this room of 8 babies with laughter, songs, music, and stories. They were generous with their hugs and in providing physical comfort, and always patient and responsive in the genuine conversations they had with babies. And, despite the atmosphere that anything can happen here, it was clear as I watched the care teachers that there was intentionality in the seeming chaos, and order among apparent disorder. These thoughtful, creative, spontaneous long-term partners in care worked seamlessly together. My words to summarize my experience in this baby room are *joyful* and *spontaneous* to capture its essence as vivid, varied, engaging, and full of fun.

Botanical Garden—Intentional and Well-Managed

A botanical garden, like the one shown in Figure 1.5, is typically on a relatively large plot of land dedicated to the growing and maintaining of plants, trees, and flowers for the purposes of the enjoyment and enrichment of people as well as for the cultivation of its plantings for scientific research. It is a place of beauty, with purposeful plantings designed by expert landscape architects. Botanical gardens have pathways directing individuals through the grounds, which twist and turn or meander along to reveal plots of plants and flowers, labeled and described, and laid out in a pattern that changes only with the passing of the seasons. The environment tells its visitors, "Enjoy the beauty in this well-organized space." Challenge: Although the reliable sameness and predictability of the garden may comfort many, others may find it overly constraining.

The Botanical Garden Baby Room was a very pleasant, comfortable, spacious, and well-ordered space full of natural light and floor to ceiling windows that looked out onto big shady trees and the play yard. The room had well-defined areas that invited different types of play (e.g., quiet, messy, and noisy) and that directed the flow of babies and adults in the room. The lead care teacher, Annie, was masterful at organizing a space that was responsive, engaging, and appropriately challenging for the 8 children in this multiage room that accepted children ages 6 weeks

Figure 1.5. A Botanical Garden

to 2 years of age. And, because of the large spread of ages, there were plenty of toys, materials, and equipment to accommodate the varying sizes, abilities, and developmental differences.

As part of a university laboratory preschool program, Annie also juggled things like schedules, assignments, assessments, and providing directions for other professional care teachers, university students, researchers, and volunteers from the community that occupied this room daily. In fact, there seemed to always be numerous adults in this baby room, all with different levels of understanding of babies and their needs. Because of this, routine and a sameness of expectations was deemed essential so that all who engaged within the space were aided in knowing what needed to be done and how they were expected to do it. I use two words to capture the essence of the Botanical Garden Baby Room, *intentional* and *well-managed* which describe how in this space, all that happens is done with thorough planning, and everything is well managed, including people, time, and materials.

Laboratory Greenhouse—Rigorous and Controlled

A laboratory greenhouse, depicted in Figure 1.6, is an enclosed structure that is specifically designed for the indoor growing of various types of plants, including fruits and vegetables, shrubs, tree saplings, and flowers. Plants that might not withstand the current weather conditions or

Figure 1.6. A Laboratory Greenhouse

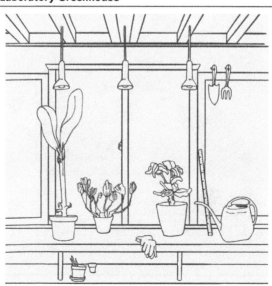

climate in nature are grown in greenhouses as well. This is sometimes referred to as *hothousing*. Other purposes of laboratory greenhouses are for researching the breeding of plants and protocols and tools for growing them, or for the genetic engineering of plants. This type of research is conducted carefully under very controlled conditions, with continuous monitoring and recording of data. This environment says, "I am in control of the outcomes here." Challenge: While this may be fascinating to some, especially some researchers, to others it may feel unnatural and even disquieting.

In the Laboratory Greenhouse Baby Room, the 8 babies in the room (ages 3 to 12 months) were carefully monitored for growth, development, and the achievement of physical and cognitive benchmarks. Each child's accomplishments in this university laboratory preschool were charted on posters that hung on the wall that also listed the next developmental step the care teachers needed to "teach" the babies (e.g., roll front to back, lift head 45 degrees, stack 3 objects). Hanging on the walls just outside the room were posters documenting research done in the room. While the room arrangement was functional, it was unattractive and uncomfortable with no place for adults to sit except on a hard, thinly carpeted floor. Further, it was cluttered and noisy, and always seemed to have lingering, unpleasant odors.

There were no professionals working in this room; rather, there were 11 different adults who interacted with babies each day. This included three undergraduate students for each of three 3-hour shifts, who were supervised by two different doctoral students who worked half-day shifts. They were all pleasant, dedicated, and appeared to really enjoy being with the babies. They followed rigid guidelines designed by a faculty supervisor years in the past that specified exactly what toys were to be put in front of babies at what time and for how long, and the exact way to position the bodies of premobile babies (i.e., back, side, front, other side, propped to stand upright). Toys and body positions were changed every 15 minutes throughout the day. I use the words *rigorous* and *controlled* for this environment, to capture its strict adherence to a predetermined schedule.

CONCLUSION

As you read this book, I invite you to reflect upon the stories of those individuals within the baby rooms—the babies, care teachers, administrators, and family members. Try to see what is described through their eyes, considering the different viewpoints they may represent. Consider how they may have lived their experiences cognitively *and* emotionally. Also, consider how the environment (Meditation Garden, Wildflower

Meadow, Botanical Garden, Laboratory Greenhouse) may have impacted the experiences, decisions, and activities that occurred. Is there something about the environment that may have contributed to the behaviors or outcomes described? How could the events have been different if they had occurred in your own setting?

CHAPTER 2

Comfort and Security

Comfort and security are essential elements to overall well-being in baby rooms, important for everyone sharing the space, adults and children alike (McCormick & McMullen, 2019; McMullen et al., 2016). To help you understand what comfort and security mean—what it *looks and feels like*—in baby rooms, I ask you to first consider the opposite. Imagine what the lived experience of adults and children in baby rooms might be like in the absence of comfort and security:

> Every day, you spend 8–9 hours, 5 days a week, in a place that makes you *uncomfortable*—physically and emotionally. The air is filled not only with bad smells, but with tension. The temperature is always too hot or too cold, and other people in the room are moody and quick to anger, or sullen and

uncommunicative. Everywhere you look you see clutter and chaos. Now, imagine you not only feel uncomfortable, but also insecure. You are frequently anxious, maybe fearful that you or someone in the space with you might get sick or injured. Maybe you and other care teachers are worried about keeping your jobs, and babies cannot trust their needs will be met in a reliable and compassionate manner.

Now, try to imagine the opposite of what I just described. Picture yourself in a baby room in which your lived experience (i.e., processed both cognitively + emotionally) fosters a sense of comfort and a sense of security. What does that look and feel like? Take a moment to describe it to yourself. While doing so, consider these questions: What would I and other adults need in this environment to feel comfortable and secure? What do the babies need?

UNDERSTANDING THE WELL-BEING SENSES OF COMFORT AND SECURITY

There are a few differences, of course, between what adults and babies may need to achieve comfort and security in baby rooms, but there are also many things in common across the age groups. I describe these senses of well-being as follows:

> *Sense of Comfort* is experienced when an individual (adult or baby) is relaxed or at ease physically and emotionally most of the time in a space. The general tone or mood is pleasant and typically without the kinds of palpable tension that accompanies negativity and conflict among individuals. Those in the space find it well-organized, thoughtfully arranged, aesthetically appealing, in short, simply a pleasant place to be. Contributing to the sense of comfort or being at ease in an environment requires having what is needed readily and reliably available. For mobile babies, this means they can freely access toys and materials; and for adults, this means they have storage for personal items and necessary supplies for themselves and babies closely within reach. Further, comfort is experienced when there are plenty of uncrowded spaces and places for adults and babies to feel relaxed, cozy, and content, with appropriately sized furniture and soft materials and flooring to sit or lie down on, or crawl or walk upon.

> *Sense of Security* is experienced when an individual (adult or baby) is generally free from worry; they believe their health and safety are protected, and they find procedures and practices stable and predictable. In this space babies have learned, and thus have developed the expectation, that their needs will be met reasonably quickly, with kindness and sensitivity by someone

who knows and understands them as individuals. Care teachers are more secure when organizational climate factors (Dennis & O'Connor, 2013; Veziroglu-Celik & Yildiz, 2018) are addressed, for instance, when employment policies provide stability and job security: when they are clear about and able to meet expectations and job requirements; and when they are regularly, reliably, and adequately compensated for what they do (Cumming, 2017; Thompson, 2014).

As you read and reflect upon the three life stories in this chapter, consider the role of the senses of comfort and security in shaping the daily lived experiences of the characters. For instance, ask yourself the following questions:

- How are the well-being senses of comfort and security enhanced or diminished by the environments, relationships, or activities/ practices in these baby rooms?
- How might they impact the capacity to care for the babies, families, and others in the environment fully, responsively, and without distraction?
- What could be done to better support comfort and security for care teachers, babies, and their families represented in these stories?
- What might be the long-term consequences for adults and children of being in this environment?

A PLACE FOR BABY *AND* MOM

Preamble

In "A Place for Baby and Mom," you meet Treshawn's mom, Keysha, who is transitioning her daughter—and herself—slowly into the Meditation Garden Baby Room. Will they be happy here after their recent failed attempts to feel comfortable and secure in two other infant childcare programs? Following the life story, I reflect on the Big Idea of "family-centered" or "whole-family" care and how it can support the comfort and security of children and their families in baby rooms.

Life Story

Despite putting her name on the waiting list for a spot in the Meditation Garden Baby Room early in her pregnancy, Keysha was disappointed to find out there was still no space available three months after her daughter, Treshawn, was born. Feeling a need to settle her childcare problem soon, she started making calls to other community childcare centers. She enrolled in one infant program, and then a second, both of which she left after just a couple of weeks. She said she found the first room "chaotic" and the care teachers "disinterested." She said she did not trust that any of the babies, including her own, were having their needs met. What she reported as "alarming" to her was that "they let them sit in dirty and wet diapers when they were clearly uncomfortable if it was not 'time' to change them." According to Keysha, little or no information was provided to families about what happened during the day, and there was "no sense of organization or routine."

In the second room, although she said she couldn't quite put her finger on what made her uncomfortable. "Everything looked okay," she said, but "it just *felt* off." She described the care teachers as "not very friendly," to either herself or her daughter, which she said was "different from how they treated other parents and babies." Although she admitted it might be because they were still new, she said she worried it might be because they were the only non-White family in the program.

With just a few short weeks left of what had been maternity leave coupled with summer vacation, Keysha was growing increasingly worried about how soon she was expected to return to her teaching job. The family could not afford for her to remain out of work indefinitely. They had no nearby family and no particularly close friends able to take care of a child so young. But then she got the call that, she said, "changed our lives." A spot had opened in the Meditation Garden Baby Room, and she was invited to enroll Treshawn, now 5-months-old. I remember her telling me that her initial reaction was to flip back-and-forth between the old adage, "Third time's a charm," and the superstition, "Bad things come in threes."

Before officially enrolling in the program, Lily Grace, one of the co-lead care teachers from the baby room, called Keysha to arrange a convenient time that she and her co-lead care teacher could come visit the family in their home. Lily Grace told her that it was so they and the family could "begin to develop a relationship" with one another and so the care teachers could get a sense of what Treshawn herself likes and dislikes. "Lily Grace explained to me," said Keysha, "that they like to mirror practices done in the home" as much as possible. According to Lily Grace, they also explained to Keysha that they wanted to discuss the family's goals for their daughter and how they could best support them while in this program.

During the home visit, Lily Grace described the nature of their continuity of care program and informed Keysha that, if they stayed in the program, they would all be working together until the summer after Treshawn turned three. Keysha told me that her first thought was, "Wow, this sounds so cool!" And then she added that this was followed closely by a second, worrying thought: "Oh no! What if they don't like us?" She and I laughed about how her glass always seemed to be half full and half empty at the same time!

The home visit happened a few days before I met Keysha and started my 3-week observation and data collection in the baby room. Early on my first morning, Lily Grace informed me that a new family, Keysha and her baby Treshawn, would be arriving to spend a couple of hours "getting comfortable in the room." Lily Grace explained that the week before she and her co-lead care teacher, Lisa, had visited them in their home, and that they planned to come for a short period today to "get a sense of the routine and the flow of the day." Today would be the first time Keysha and Treshawn would see the room.

Soon after, I noticed the door of the baby room opening slowly. I saw what I assumed to be Keysha, toting Treshawn by the handle of her car seat–carrier as she entered rather hesitantly. Lily Grace calmly rose from her position on the carpet to greet them. She went up to them, and with a beautiful warm smile and melodic voice, she said, "Welcome, Keysha." And turning her gaze directly to the baby, she clapped her hands together softly, and said, "Oh, oh, oh, my, it is so good to see you again, Treshawn." And, touching the baby's cheek gently with the back of her hand, Lily Grace added, "Oh, my, you are such a sweet girl, aren't you!? I am so happy you have arrived. Can I pick you up and show you the room?" Baby Treshawn beamed a smile that lit up her whole face as Lily Grace unstrapped her from her car seat and picked her up. Mom Keysha visibly relaxed and, smiling shyly, said, "We're so happy to be here. Thank you."

Keysha and Treshawn stayed only 2 hours that 1st day, but with each new day, mother and baby stayed a bit longer. On Friday, they stayed for 6 hours, nearly a whole day. I talked to Lily Grace about this, wondering if it was common for a family member to stay with their child so long when they were transitioning into her baby room. "No, not typical, but it happens. Every situation is different. Whatever she [the mother] needs to do to feel comfortable and to come to trust us is fine." Laughing quietly, she remarked that in her experience (over 20 years), she found parents sometimes had more difficulty with "big" transitions than their children, like when beginning the program or transitioning to preschool. Becoming thoughtful, and rather serious, she went on to share her thoughts that she needed to take "particular care," in developing her relationships with Keysha and Treshawn, because, she said, "Keysha's sense of trust in childcare has been damaged by her previous two bad experiences."

Although wanting to proceed cautiously and not rush her, Lily Grace expressed awareness and concern that Keysha would soon be returning to work full-time. She told me that she saw it was part of her role as the family's key care teacher to help lead both mother and baby toward greater independence from one another over the next couple of weeks. To this end, I observed how during the family's 2nd week in the baby room, Lily Grace asked Keysha to "be a helper" in the room (e.g, picking up toys, cleaning tables, warming bottles). It wasn't long before Keysha, following Lily Grace's lead, began to engage with babies other than just her own daughter by talking and singing, bottle and spoon feeding, rocking and hugging, and supporting and encouraging play. Lily Grace told me that she thought it was a good idea for Keysha to help, not only so Treshawn could interact in the environment more independently, but so Keysha would come to know and trust in the routines and caregiving practices in which they engaged in this room. Baby Treshawn, for her part, was just fine with this new arrangement and seemed delighted in everything and everybody in the baby room, including the other care teachers and babies.

Halfway through this 2nd week, Lily Grace began encouraging Keysha to leave the room, inviting her to "go take a walk" or "go run some errands." Keysha did this, steadily increasing the amount of time she was away. She always looked satisfied and thrilled to see how happy Treshawn was upon her return and to hear what she had been doing. Keysha and Lily Grace set up a plan for their 3rd week: mom would leave Treshawn all morning on Monday and Tuesday, and then try to stay away the whole day beginning on Wednesday. I'm happy to say the plan seemed to work out well for everyone. Several weeks after Keysha and Treshawn had fully transitioned into the room, and a while after I had completed my research there, I learned from Lily Grace that, "all was going well." Treshawn's father dropped her off a bit before 8:00 a.m. every morning, and Keysha came to pick her up sometime after 4:30 every afternoon. According to Lily Grace, Keysha enjoyed "hanging out" in the baby room or on the playground at the end of the day with several other moms and one dad who picked their kids up around the same time. She said they seemed to enjoy talking and laughing together about their work lives and the joys and challenges of raising very young children.

Reflection—Family-Centered, Whole-Family Care

I will always treasure the times I have spent in the Meditation Garden Baby Room, especially because it is such a treat to see Lily Grace in action. I had the privilege of observing her work in this continuity of care program, following her progress as she "looped" through several cycles with each group of infants, who became toddlers and then 2-year-olds, before she helped transition them and their families into preschool. I was inspired by how this quiet, kind, and humble woman lived out the deep and abiding respect that she so clearly had for each and every baby, family, and staff member with whom she worked.

Over the years, I and so many others (e.g., her coworkers, university students, researchers) have learned many important lessons from Lily Grace. One of those key learnings, for me, is demonstrated in the story just shared—how the baby *and* the family is the unit of care in baby rooms. Lily Grace exemplified what it means to care for the *whole* family by engaging in what are typically described as "family-centered practices" (Gonzalez-Mena, 2012; Keyser, 2017). In the ECCE field, we have borrowed the definition of family-centered practices from our colleagues in special education and early intervention (Dunst et al., 2019; Pianta et al., 2012; Ziviani et al., 2011). According to the National Resource Center for Family Centered Practice (n.d.):

> Family centered practice is based upon the belief that the best way to meet a person's [child's or baby's] needs is within their families [by providing] services that engage, involve, strengthen, and support families. The family-centered model, which views families as having the capacity to make informed decisions and act on them, differs from models in which professionals make decisions alone. [Instead, they engage] with family members to understand their lives, goals, strengths, and challenges, [thereby] developing a relationship between family and practitioner. (para. 1)

It has always been my conviction, which I try to convey to future teachers, that in childcare for birth- to 3-year-olds, as professionals, we work with both the children and their family members. I stress that although working with or involving families is important throughout childhood, it is a critical necessity for professionals in infant/toddler care and education. In McMullen (2013), I described this whole family approach as a "Guiding Principle of Practice" in childcare with infants and toddlers that compels us to:

> Partner fully with families in caring for their children . . . by respecting families as partners, not clients or customers, and recognize their expertise by honoring the decisions they make about their infants and toddlers . . . families should feel empowered and their capacity to support their child's development bolstered. (p. 26)

My support for family-centered practices was affirmed and strengthened when I observed Lily Grace. In "A Place for Baby and Mom," we see how Lily Grace's adoption of family-centeredness as a basic principle of her practice made a very real difference in the lives of baby Treshawn and her mother Keysha. Lily Grace showed families she valued getting to know them and their babies at the very beginning of their 3-year journeys together by doing home visits. She demonstrated her desire to empower Keysha's capacity to support her own needs as well as those of her baby both by involving her in the day-to-day life in the baby room and by working with her on a plan for transitioning into full-time care.

To support comfort and security, Lily Grace and the other members of her care team (co-lead care teacher and teachers' aides) went beyond welcoming, including, and/or involving family members in their babies' care, as important as all of those things are—they incorporated family members into the care team as important and contributing members.

Invitation for Further Reflection and Discussion

1. How did this story make you feel? Can you personally relate to any of the characters?
2. How do you transition families into your room? Do you think it works well? What would you change if you could?
3. If you were a parent of a baby in this room, do you think you would be comfortable with the idea of a home visit from the lead care teachers before beginning the program? If you were one of the care teachers, would you be comfortable going into the homes of the families who have just enrolled in the program, assuming they are strangers to you?
4. What would you have done if you were the key care teacher in this story and you had a family member staying all day with their child like Keysha did? What might you have done differently to make mom feel comfortable and secure?
5. What is your philosophy about families in your room or program? How do you feel about how I have described family-centered or whole-family care?
6. Are you comfortable with how much Lily Grace and her team emphasize care practices mirroring what families do at home? Is that always possible? Why or why not? How do you balance what the family wants and realities in your program?

THROUGH THE LOOKING GLASS

Preamble

In "Through the Looking Glass," I share the story of my encounter with a mother, Paola, in an observation booth as we watched her 3-month-old daughter, Mila, sob on the floor of the Laboratory Greenhouse Baby Room, seemingly ignored by everyone in the room. I consider my ethical and moral responsibility in this situation as it relates to being a visitor or guest who is there to observe and do research. Following the story, I reflect on the Big Idea of how sensitively responsive care is needed to support comfort and security.

Life Story

It was Friday, the end of the 1st week of the 2 that I would spend in the Laboratory Greenhouse Baby Room, and I was very much looking forward to the break I hoped the weekend would provide. It was also nearing the end of the morning; "Phew," I remember thinking, "I'm almost halfway through." This was a difficult observation site, and this morning, although typical in many ways of the others I'd experienced that week, was one of the hardest days so far: lots of fussy and disengaged babies; lots of hubbub caused by the endless toing and froing of care teachers; and lots of my feeling anxious and confused by what I was seeing. When noon finally arrived, I was emotionally drained and ready for a break. I grabbed my backpack and headed into the soundproof observation booth just outside the baby room so I could continue to watch and take notes while I ate lunch.

As I sat down to eat, my attention was drawn to one of the room's youngest babies lying on her back on a playmat just outside the one-way mirror of the observation booth. I watched as she started to get a little fussy. Before long, her fussiness became a full-blown cry which eventually escalated into one of those heavy, gasping-for-breath kinds of sobs. All my instincts screamed, "Do something!" I pictured myself running into the room, scooping her up in my arms, holding her securely against my chest, cheek-to-cheek, with one hand cradling the back of her head, rocking her gently back and forth while whispering, "Shhh shhhh shhh shhh, it'll be okay, baby, I'm here sweet girl, I'm here, that's right, shhh, shhh, shhh, shhh." Instead, I watched anxiously as the three care teachers on duty carried on frenetically with their routines, ignoring the crying baby completely, and walking straight past her numerous times without a glance. For that matter, none of the other babies seemed to notice the sobbing of their peer either. "How very strange," I wrote in my field notes, "No one is taking any notice." My appetite was gone; my lunch was left half eaten.

I was so lost in my concern that I did not hear the door to the observation booth open. From somewhere behind me, I heard a woman say, with some alarm, "Oh my God. Is she all right? Aren't they going to pick her up? Why aren't they helping her?!?" I introduced myself and told her what I was doing there, and I soon learned the woman's name was Paola and the distraught baby alone on the baby room floor was her 3-month-old daughter, Mila. "How long has this been going on?" asked Paola in a quivering voice. "For at least 5 minutes now," I replied. I could feel that she wanted to rush right into the room, but hesitated because, "she wasn't supposed to." Although families were invited to go into the observation room anytime they wished, they were asked to only come into the baby room at drop-off and pick-up times, and then they were to remain in the small, crowded entry area.

Every time I think about that day, the horrible moments that Paola and I stood side-by-side watching her baby through that one-way window, I can still hear Mila's shrill cry and desperate sobs. To me, she was screaming, "Please, help me." Why could no one else hear this desperate call except for her mother and me? The episode haunts me to this day, the emotions so vivid that the helplessness I felt in that moment washes over me as I write this.

You may be wondering why I did not go to baby Mila, as my instincts compelled me. Honestly, I still feel like a coward when I think about it, but like Mila's mother, I hesitated. I had been told in no uncertain terms that I was *not* to pick up a crying baby; in fact, I was not to pick up any baby in the Laboratory Greenhouse Baby Room, except in an emergency. This rule was not just for me as a guest doing research, but rather it was the philosophy of the program: (1) Do not pick up, hold, and/or carry babies unless it is to move them from one place to another; and (2) let babies "cry it out" for a minimum of 20 minutes before attempting to calm them down with any physical contact. Their theory was that babies would come to depend too much upon adults to comfort them and that they would stop being "criers" when they learned that adults would not respond. This was a requirement set down by the researchers from the academic unit related to this birth- to age 5 preschool who were studying how to "extinguish" crying in babies, among other behaviors they wanted to learn to manage and control.

All that, and more, ran quickly through my mind as I faced Paola and considered her next question, asked after I explained I was an early childhood professor and that I study babies in childcare. "Is this what *you* would do?" Paola demanded. I felt cornered. On the one hand, I felt, as a guest, that I had no business telling Paola what I thought *should* happen; on the other hand, I felt I had a moral and ethical obligation to tell the truth as I saw it. "Welllllll," I stammered, at least at first. "No, it's not what I would do." Feeling a bit stronger now that the cat was out of the bag, I continued more emphatically, "I believe in responding to babies as quickly as possible when they cry, that a cry is a communication of some kind of need."

Well, I knew I was in trouble. Paola, seeming to find affirmation and strength in what I said, turned on her heels and left the observation booth. Next, through the glass, I saw her pick Mila up gently, but quickly, off the floor and, well, she did almost exactly what I had envisioned myself doing—what almost any of us might have done instinctively. She held Mila in her arms, against her chest, cheek-to-cheek, with one hand cradling the back of her head, and she rocked her gently back and forth and whispered, "Shhh shhhh shhh shhh, it'll be okay, Mommy's here, you'll be all right, shhh, shhh, shhh, shhh." As Mila calmed, Paola turned to the nearest care teacher and said, emphatically, "I'm taking Mila home."

Not too long after this, and certainly not very surprisingly, the director of the program sent a message that I was to come and see her in her office immediately. When I got there, she told me that Paola had visited her shortly after leaving the baby room. Apparently, Paola had sat in the director's office and cried and told the director what she had seen and how unhappy she was, as she rocked Mila, who had fallen asleep in her arms. The director was not pleased with me, to say the least. She reminded me that I was an observer, and in that role, it was their expectation that I was there to learn about them—not to "interfere" in any way. "Fair enough," I remember thinking. I apologized to the director for "interfering" (echoing her own word). I did not, however, apologize for telling Mila's mother what I really believed about their policy of "letting babies cry it out." After a reminder to just be a fly on the wall, I was told I was welcome back the next week as long as I did not speak to parents other than in greeting.

My second week was much the same as the first, although I was very careful to avoid speaking to or even making eye contact with any family members. Almost always, some baby, somewhere, was crying—on the play mat, from their crib, while outside on a blanket on the lawn. Again, they were nearly always virtually ignored, except on a few notable occasions. After what I came to think of as the 20-minute "care embargo" was lifted and it was clear a baby was just not going to stop crying, the care teachers did employ strategies to get them to stop. These were apparently techniques approved by someone higher up, like their graduate student supervisor, the director, or one of the professors who were said to have created this program. These methods still did not involve physical touch or holding. Sometimes they would kneel near a crying baby and try to talk to them in a soft voice. Other times they would start singing loudly right into a baby's ear (often the college fight song!). Other techniques they used to interrupt the crying included trying to startle a crying baby by shaking a rattle vigorously very near their face or slamming their hands down hard and repeatedly on the floor on either side of a baby's head. Sometimes they puffed air in their faces.

I did not fault the "care teachers" in this room for their lack of responsiveness to babies' cries; they were using methods they had been taught. They were all young college students earning a grade in a course and were expected to do as they were told. At the same time, I was alarmed and disturbed to see how easily natural instincts hardwired in our brains to trigger caring responses to babies' cries (Boukydis & Burgess, 1982; DeAngelis, 2008; National Institutes of Health, 2013) could be replaced by rigidly imposed guidelines that forced what to me were unnatural behaviors and responses. Granted, there are those who believe that there is no harm in letting babies "cry it out," that in doing so, they learn to self-soothe. Others believe too quickly responding to crying babies will "spoil" them. But it was not these or other cultural variations in beliefs being played out in this baby room. Rather it was a behavioral science experiment designed to see how much time was needed to extinguish the cries of young infants—one of their only means of communication.

Letting a baby "cry it out" for a few minutes at home is different from loud consistent crying in childcare. Even if one believes a crying baby will eventually stop on their own and learn to comfort themselves, what are we teaching the other babies by ignoring one of their peers in distress? In this case, sadly, the instincts of the babies themselves to notice and respond to the cries of other babies—what many consider the roots or very beginnings of displays of empathy—were thwarted. Although I never grew comfortable with what I was seeing, at some point during the second week, I realized that like these babies, I had become numb to the crying. I was able to ignore it. When I have reflected on this before, I have compared it to a time when my husband and I lived right next to busy train tracks. After a time, although I know we heard the trains, they barely registered; they were just part of life. It is my endless shame that this is how the babies' cries became to me.

Although I only had a sketchy idea of what happened in the director's office that afternoon in terms of her encounter with Paola, I do know that Mila was not in the baby room during my second week. I like to imagine that Paola either decided to keep her at home or sought alternative care for Mila in a place in which care teachers were professionals whose knowledge base included the concept of sensitive responsiveness. I hoped it was a place that allowed human beings to listen to their own instinctive urges to care for and respond respectfully to crying infants.

Reflection—Sensitively Responsive Care

There were many aspects of this baby room that made it difficult for those within it—including this researcher—to experience well-being that arises from senses of comfort and security. The main Big Idea for me as I think about this story is sensitively responsive care, that is, responding promptly and attentively (Elicker et al., 2014; Lally & Mangione, 2008; Wittmer & Honig, 2020). This means care teachers respond to the needs communicated through babies' cries. And that is exactly what crying is—communication (Adamson, 2018; Zero to Three, 2016). Ignoring a baby's cries increases or prolongs whatever discomfort they may be experiencing in that moment. At the same time, being ignored impacts their sense of security in terms of attachment to key care teachers in the baby room (Mann & Carney, 2008). As you may be aware, the security of attachment of babies with family members and other key care teachers can impact them well into the future. Feelings of self-worth, their ability to form trusting relationships, and their regulation of emotions, among a host of many other indicators important to healthy overall social–emotional development, are at risk (O'Connor & McCartney, 2007; Sroufe, 2005). Strong, positive, sensitively responsive care fosters secure attachment relationships between care teachers and babies that support their healthy growth, development, and well-being (Bowlby, 2007; Drugli & Undheim, 2011; Honig, 2002; Kim, 2016; Pilarza & Hill, 2014; Zeanah, 2019).

Sensitively responsive care requires listening to what babies are communicating through their cries or other verbal utterances, as well as nonverbally in terms of body language. It involves taking all communications seriously by responding as promptly as possible with kindness and respect (Dunst & Kassow, 2008; Gerber & Johnson, 2002; Horm et al., 2018; McMullen & McCormick, 2016; Ruprecht et al., 2015). It requires entering into a dialogue with a baby, what Raikes and Edwards (2009) called the "dance" that occurs between a sensitively responsive care adult and child. The back-and-forth nature of this dance or dialogue is something I tried to capture in an earlier writing (McMullen, 2013):

> Young infants need to feel secure and see the world as a trustworthy place—when I am hungry, someone feeds me; when I am sad, lonely, or scared, someone comforts me; when I am wet and uncomfortable, someone responds promptly; and those who take care of me do this with love and tenderness. To build a storehouse of trust, young infants' needs must be met predictably, promptly, and by sensitively responsive practitioners who know them well. (p. 25)

"Knowing them well" enhances the dance for both partners—adult and child. Being sensitively responsive requires providing an individualized response, one specific to each baby, rather than a one-size-fits-all strategy like pounding on the floor beside them or puffing air onto their face. It requires a matching of emotional response, one in which the care teacher empathizes with the baby or enters an intersubjective space.

Invitation for Further Reflection and Discussion

1. How did this story make you feel? Did it make you uncomfortable? Explain?

2. What would you have done if you had been in my situation as a guest or visitor to this baby room? Would you have gone into the room to comfort Baby Mila? Would you have felt a need to leave this setting?
3. What is your philosophy about comforting or responding to crying babies? When is it (or is it ever) appropriate to let them "cry it out"?
4. Although babies will eventually "cry it out," when they reach a level of exhaustion and just simply cannot continue, what lesson are they learning about themselves, others, and the world around them when this is the case?
5. What lessons were other babies in this room likely to learn about what it means to "care"?
6. Is comforting a baby something that comes naturally to a professional care teacher or something that must be learned? What do you think?
7. Sometimes care teachers may want to help a baby work through an issue or a challenge that you and her family want tackled—like giving up a pacifier or leaving comfort items at home or in a cubby. How is something like this dealt with in a sensitively responsive manner?

WHEN NOT JUST ANYONE WILL DO

Preamble

Before I did my observations in the Botanical Garden Baby Room, I had always thought that, in general, the more adults in a baby room the better. More adults meant more pairs of eyes and ears, more hands for holding children, and more attention that could be given to individual children, right? In "When Not Just Anyone Will Do," I explore how observing Enrique and others in his room led me to consider the Big Idea of key person care models and to ask the question, "Can you have *too many* adults in a baby room?"

Life Story

After spending my first few days as a researcher in the Botanical Garden Baby Room, I felt I had a sense of the daily routine and of the general personalities and temperaments of the babies in this multiage program. I really enjoyed seeing the range of development in the children altogether in one space, from those barely crawling to those who confidently walked, ran, climbed, danced, and jumped their way through the day. The one thing I wasn't quite getting a handle on was who does what and when, as far as the numerous adults in this space were concerned. There seemed to be so many big bodies among the babies, and it was taking me some time to sort them out.

In addition to family members who mostly came and went, adults in the baby room included Annie, the lead care teacher; two assistant care teachers—Danielle, who was there all day, and Serena, who worked just in the afternoons; several different undergraduate students present for a few hours each day at different times to fulfill college course requirements; a cook who delivered meals; the director who dropped in from time-to-time; researchers, like myself; and occasionally, volunteers from the community. I was told that primary care teachers (key persons) were assigned to each child and family in this continuity of care program, spread among the three paid staff members. In addition, each college student who came in had their own small primary care group for a particular day. If I was feeling confused about how all this was managed, I began to wonder about how the 8 children in this room dealt with it all. "Would just anyone do?" when it came to finding an adult to address their needs and support their interests?

As if to help me answer that question, at lunchtime that day, I had a chance to see how at least one little boy, 14-month-old Enrique, understood "who was who" and perhaps, "who mattered" in this sea of adults. Enrique was seated in a small wooden chair, just his size, pulled up close to the table top. He had on a rather large plastic bib that seemed to keep getting in his way as he picked up various pieces and parts of his lunch with his fingers. I noticed a couple of bustling adults who were busy serving children and responding to lots of expressions, verbal and nonverbal, for "more, please." Twice during this episode, an adult walked past Enrique, picked up his spork, put it in his hands, and encouraged him, very nicely, to use it to scoop up his sauce-covered pasta and his applesauce. Both times the spork was quickly abandoned, as Enrique seemed to find it more efficient, and certainly more fun, to eat his messy meal with his hands.

As I watched, Enrique's enjoyment in his lunch very suddenly was shattered as he bit down hard, not on his pasta, but on one of his fingers. He looked, first very surprised, and then alarmed as he examined his finger. He cried out sharply, but only briefly. I jumped up to see if I could help him, as did at least two other adults who came to his aid. "No!" He made it very clear that none of us was wanted. Although sniffling and lips quivering, Enrique stoically withheld his tears, but it was clear he was dreadfully sad and in pain. Turning first one way, then another, and then yet another, he finally spotted Annie across the room. As soon as the two made eye contact, Enrique let loose with big tears and a loud cry, as he held his very red, sore-looking finger up for Annie to see. Thankfully,

Annie's arms were soon wrapped around him, and her soothing words and a handy ice pack that was passed to her by a nearby student seemed to do the trick and make Enrique feel better.

The incident with Enrique led me to start observing interactions among the children and the various adults in the room more closely. The Botanical Garden Baby Room is a big, open, and spacious room; thus even with extra bodies, there was no issue of crowding. For the most part, children seemed to ignore all the extra adults, or to just accept them, or maybe to have grown used to the situation. In fact, there seemed to be many times when "any adult *would* do," like when serving food, helping them zip up coats and put on hats to go outside, getting them toys or other materials, and even when it came to sitting on a lap to read a book. But there were other times when children clearly showed a preference for a trusted and well-known key care teacher, mostly around the handling of "big emotions" like being in pain, feeling angry or sad, or when extremely overwrought with frustration. This was also true for several of the babies when it came to intimate caregiving times like diaper changing and preparing for sleep.

Over the 2 full weeks of observing in this room I came to conclude that as long as the key care teachers were there, the babies were generally unbothered by the presence of so many lesser-known grownups. The extra adults were mostly kind, positive, and helpful to the children. The babies seemed to largely benefit, in this particular space, from all the extra people to play with them, to read to them, and to feed them. But I then wondered about the professional care teachers themselves. How did they view this situation? Did *they* think there were too many adults in the room?

The lead care teacher Annie was a dedicated, knowledgeable, and highly competent professional with several years of experience behind her, but she was also quite young. She was always the youngest adult in the room, except for the students. She had herself been one of those undergraduate students in this very same baby room not too many years before. She laughed about how different it was to be on the "other side," and wondered how the lead teacher at the time, now retired, but remaining a good friend, "had ever put up with them" when she was an undergraduate. "We were so naive, so raw and rough around the edges. Full of ideas about how things 'should' be done,'" she said. Then, looking pensive, she remarked that one of the assistant care teachers she worked with now (and supervised) had also been in this room when she was a student. "That," I thought, "must be uncomfortable."

Although Annie said she "loved working with the children and their families," she said it was hard to "manage all the adults." This was especially true since most of these adults were older, and although not as well educated about young children as she, in some cases they had more years of experience. Annie worked in the baby room only in the mornings and spent the afternoons in a nearby office. She did not seem to particularly enjoy this aspect of her work, which largely consisted of doing paperwork and meeting with college students to provide feedback on assignments and their practices when in the baby room. "Add to that," she said, "there are the volunteers. Most of them are very nice and well-meaning," but, she went on to explain, they "rarely know much about young children and how to talk to them, at least not the way we want them to!"

As an example, Annie reminded me of an incident from that very morning. Mrs. J., an older retiree from another department at the university, wanted to start coming in as a volunteer one morning a week. She was a generous donor to the program, in acknowledgement of her grandchildren who had attended a few years before. Today was her first day, and while she was there, I had observed a very patient, but clearly frustrated, Annie try to gently guide and sometimes directly intervene to correct Mrs. J.'s tendency to, as Annie said, "do too much for" the children. I had noted in my journal how Mrs. J had been harsh and negative in her words and actions with the babies. "Geeze," said Annie, "What am I going to do?! How do I, a 20-something, tell a 70-something grandmother that she is, 'not doing it right'?" How indeed, I wondered, feeling inadequate to advise her. I recorded in my notes that I was going to have to give much thought to how I might do a better job preparing my young future care teachers for a position like Annie's.

When I talked to them later, Danielle and Serena, the two assistant care teachers, echoed Annie's concerns about dealing with so many other adults in the baby room. "It is hard sometimes," said Serena, who was a very positive person, and who during my time there never spoke a negative or unkind word about anyone or anything. "But we're here to help others learn what's best for babies and young children." Danielle was blunter, "It's *impossible*. We're mentoring and monitoring so many people that it distracts from our work with the kids!"

Reflection—Key Persons

Diebold and Perren (2019) are among many researchers who have asserted that large group sizes and having too few adults per child contributes to lower quality of interactions between adults and babies. This is something I think we have largely accepted as a given in ECCE, at least in the United States, for decades. But in the preamble to the story, I took a new spin on the question of ratios and group sizes, asking the question, "Can you have *too many* adults in a baby room?" Katsiada et al. (2018) suggested that you can. Their research team found that the larger the number of adults in baby rooms, the higher the incidence of inconsistency in care responses (Pauker et al., 2018), the lower the level of collaboration among adults, and the greater the frequency of adults talking to other adults. Further, they found that extra adults in baby rooms often lacked the qualifications and understanding of how to work with children this age.

One important consideration in determining the answer is whether the room is big enough for all the children and adults to engage without crowding. As I described, the Botanical Garden Baby Room was spacious and open, made to feel even more so by its large windows and abundance of natural light. I never felt it was overcrowded with people when I was there; I just felt a bit confused by what seemed like a surplus of adults for the number of babies. Having extra adults on hand certainly seems like it would be helpful in a baby room. But is it? Or was it, in this case? The care teachers in this room raised my concern about this when they complained about how time-consuming and potentially distracting it was to have to manage adult behaviors.

But the Big Idea this experience led me to was about the need for key persons and what that really means in a situation like this. As I pointed out in the story, Enrique and the other children seemed to willingly accept the help of the "extra" adults when they were doing things like preparing and giving them food, providing a comfy lap to read them their favorite books, or picking up toys and tidying the space around them. But, when it came to needs related to big feelings and intimate care moments, such as diaper changing or attending to a boo-boo, the babies wanted someone that they knew and trusted and who knew them well. It was these key persons who were able to help them regain an equilibrium in terms of comfort and security. In other words, these persons represented what is known as a "secure-base," among attachment theorists (Balaban, 2006; Ereky-Stevens et al., 2018; Honig, 2002; Opie et al., 2021). But in such a large group, could Enrique and the other children always find their key person(s) among the vast sea of adult bodies when they needed them most?

My concern of children being able to find their key persons led me to consider adult/child ratios and group size. As readers know, and I indicated before, we have long held in American ECCE that the more adults who are available per child, the better, in terms of positive experiences and outcomes for children, as long as the overall size of the group remains low. In a systematic review of this issue, Dalgaard et al. (2020) affirmed that ratios and group sizes affect

> the process characteristics of quality of care, meaning that an increased adult/
> child ratio and reduced group size are associated with an increase in positive
> child–caretaker interaction and in caretaker sensitivity, responsiveness,
> warmth, nurture and encouragement towards the children [and] associated
> with positive cognitive, behavioral and socioemotional child outcomes. (p. 3)

The implications of existing research, like that done by Dalgaard and her colleagues, is based upon the assumption that the adults in the adult/child ratio are the "right" adults, the ones able to engage in the positive interactions that lead to such positive outcomes. Bjørnestad and her colleagues in Norway (2020) recently concluded that the quality of the care teachers' interactions with toddlers varies across different adults in settings. From all this I conclude, *not just anyone will do*. At least, not for the really important interpersonal stuff.

So, returning to the Big Idea of this story, my main takeaway is how very important certain key persons are to very young children. It forced me to reevaluate my initial understandings of the meaning of key persons (McCormick et al., 2021). The practice of assigning key persons is much more than a structural matter. *Structural factors* are those things that are predetermined, regulated, written down, and so on (Cassidy et al., 2005; Phillips et al., 2000; Slot, 2018) often before care teachers and children and families have any knowledge of one another or any trusting relationships have begun to form. Clearly, key persons are those individuals who engage in relational aspects of care with babies which is related to *process* not structure (de Schipper et al., 2004; Slot, 2018). I realize now more than ever that structure and process are both very important in influencing relationships between care teachers and babies (Burchinal, 2018; Dalli et al., 2011; Recchia & Shin, 2012; Vandell, 1996). This was a case where the structural component that allowed a large group size was in danger of overwhelming the relational processes.

For the babies in this room, a key person was someone *they*, the babies, sought out and relied upon, a familiar adult with whom they had formed a relationship. It was someone whom they trusted to calm and soothe them in their most difficult moments. As care teacher Vivian, from the Wildflower Meadow Baby Room told me in an interview, years later, when it comes to key persons, "The babies choose us."

Invitation for Further Reflection and Discussion

1. Can you relate to any of the characters in this story?
2. How does what is described in the story relate to the well-being senses of comfort and security?
3. Have you ever been a child's "key person" whether officially assigned or not? If so, how did it work? In your opinion, what are the pros and cons of formalizing the assignment of a care teacher to certain specific children and their families as the official key person?
4. What did Annie mean when she said the volunteer tended to "do too much for" the children?

5. How would you answer the question, "Can you have too many adults in a childcare room?" If you answer yes, how many is too many? How do you determine this?
6. If you were a professional care teacher in a room that opens its doors to nonprofessionals (e.g., students, volunteers, families, researchers), do you feel prepared to manage them? If so, how were you prepared? Should preparation for managing adults be part of what future care teachers learn in early childhood professional preparation programs?
7. How do you think it might impact your attention to the children and their families if you were managing multiple adults in a setting? Have you ever experienced this, or any other factors that divided your attention? What was that like?

CONCLUSION

In this chapter I presented the senses of comfort and security as necessary for the well-being of the babies and adults who spend their days in baby rooms. I described a sense of comfort as occurring when an individual is relaxed and at ease physically and emotionally, and a sense of security being experienced when one is free of worry, believes their health and safety are protected, and finds things to be stable and predictable. I reflected on ways that comfort and security are supported (or not) by considering the Big Ideas of family-centered, whole-family care; sensitive responsiveness; and key person care. Along the way, I have asked several questions and provided prompts for you to reflect upon and, hopefully, provoke discussion with your colleagues.

CHAPTER 3

Belonging, Respect, and Communication

Big or small, to be and feel well, all humans have a fundamental need to love and be loved, to feel they are cared for by others, and to be able to express their own natural intuition to care. These needs motivate individuals to seek out relationships with those around them. In baby rooms, positive and trusting relationships between and among babies, their families, and care teachers promote their lived experiences of belonging, respect, and communication needed for well-being to flourish. In addition, a climate of inclusivity is a necessary ingredient to achieving these senses of well-being. Respect borne of a spirit of inclusivity fosters the formation of relationships that honor the dignity and uniqueness of each individual—baby or adult—for who they are. This includes who they are within their families, cultures, and communities; their ways of communicating; and how their identities intersect with race, gender, religion, developmental or physical disability, and socioeconomic status (Doucet, 2019; Goodwin et al., 2008; Souto-Manning & Rabadi-Raol, 2018).

UNDERSTANDING THE WELL-BEING SENSES OF BELONGING, RESPECT, AND COMMUNICATION

There is a general way to understand the highly related well-being senses of belonging, respect, and communication, as well as specific considerations for meeting those needs in the adults versus children in baby rooms. These three important elements of well-being are defined briefly below, followed by further elaboration of their meaning in adults and babies.

Sense of Belonging is experienced when an individual perceives and feels connected to those around them in the baby room, feeling that they are a member of a community that is a friendly place in which they can enjoy being with their peers or colleagues. Care teachers in baby rooms are more likely to thrive and experience well-being when they sense collegiality and a belonging to a larger community of practice with their care team and others in their setting (McGinty et al., 2008; McMullen et al., 2020; Thorpe et al., 2020; Wesley & Buysse, 2001). Babies also begin to develop their own sense of collegiality in early experiences with peers, building expectations from those they find friendly, fun, and interesting (Shin, 2010; Waldman, 2005). Babies receive strong messages from others, in particular their care teachers, about who is deemed more (or less) worthy of belonging in the group, including themselves, through direct experience with care teachers and by observing the care teachers' interactions with their peers (Derman-Sparks & Edwards, 2020; Doucet, 2019; Lally & Mangione, 2008; McMullen & Apple, 2012; Raikes & Edwards, 2009).

Sense of Respect is experienced when an individual has positive thoughts and feelings about themselves because their personal attributes, beliefs, culture, and family are acknowledged, honored, and valued by others in the setting. Further, it is experienced when individuals believe they are free to express themselves if their sense of self-respect has been violated, intentionally or not, by others, and that they can do so without risk of harm, retribution, or ostracization by others. Adult care teachers experience well-being associated with respect if they, as the unique individuals they are, feel they are acknowledged, appreciated, and accepted—not merely tolerated—by their professional colleagues, the families of the children in their room, and the childcare community at large (Goouch & Powell, 2013; McDonald et al., 2018; Roberts et al., 2019; Thorpe et al., 2020). Babies learn important early and life-lasting lessons from the respect shown for their bodies, individual temperaments, and preferences, as well as for their families and culture by the care teachers and other adults in the baby room (Cárcamo et al., 2016; Shirvanian & Michael, 2017).

Sense of Communication is experienced when an individual knows and feels they are understood, verbally and nonverbally, by others who actively listen and respond appropriately and predictably. Communication that impacts the well-being of those in baby rooms involves multiple players and layers; it occurs between and among adult care teachers, family members, and babies and their peers, as well as staff colleagues, administrators, and sometimes other community members who have reason to interact with those in the baby room. At its core, the need to understand and be understood by others is a human need, regardless of the person's age. While this is true, some adults have more difficulty understanding and appreciating the communications of preverbal babies (Valloton, 2009), sometimes disregarding their ability to be communication partners either because of a lack of knowledge about how babies communicate or feeling embarrassed at "talking" to babies (McMullen & Brody, 2021).

Trusting relationships among individuals must be built over time as knowledge of one another grows and bonds are strengthened. To this end, the birth-to-3 profession widely endorses practices designed to support positive and trusting relationships between and among babies, care teachers, and families. Such relational practices include continuity of care (McMullen, 2013; Zero to Three, 2010), the assignment of primary (or key person) care teachers (Bernhardt, 2000; Cryer et al., 2000; McMullen, 2018; McMullen et al., 2015), and family-centered practices (Douglass, 2011; Dunst et al., 2019; Gonzalez-Mena, 2012; Keyser, 2017; Pianta et al., 2012). The long-term and committed relationships fostered by such practices allow care teachers to develop a depth of knowledge of the unique and individual nature of the babies in their care and of their families (i.e., culture, values, goals for their children, and so on). Such strong relationships allow care teachers to respond to each baby's communications of needs and desires appropriately and sensitively and to support the goals and values held by the baby's family.

In the three life stories below, consider how belonging, respect, and communication impact the lived experience of the featured characters. Ask yourself these questions while reading:

- How are the well-being senses of belonging, respect, and communication, as I defined them above, enhanced or diminished by the environments, relationships, or activities/practices in these baby rooms?
- What could be done to better support belonging, respect, and communication in each of these instances?
- What consequences, positive or negative, might result for the adults and children in the situations described in the stories?

A HUNDRED LANGUAGES IN BABY ROOMS

Preamble

This is a composite story of my lived experiences in three settings, including the Meditation Garden, Wildflower Meadow, and Botanical Garden baby rooms. My focus in the story is on the amazing capabilities of babies as communicators and the different practices I saw to support this. In addition to care teacher practices, I provide an example of how the environment itself can speak to babies. As you read this story, think about your own style of communicating with babies. Have you ever underestimated them as communication partners? As both givers and receivers of messages in your environment? After the story, I reflect upon the meaning of "100 languages in baby rooms" and my support for the United Nations (2009) Convention on the Rights of the Child, as it relates to what I have identified as a Big Idea behind this story, that all children have the right to be heard and understood.

Life Story

As I positioned myself on the floor for the start of that day's observation in the baby room, I thought about the advice I give my students who are going to spend time with babies and care teachers. I tell them to try to keep their eyes, ears, and heart as open as possible, to be mindful and in the moment. "Just allow yourself to 'be,' and try to experience the moments as the children do." I tried to follow my own advice. The first person to catch my eye was Jesse, one of the two co-lead care teachers, as she exited the changing room carrying Brad. I watched and I listened as, with a sing-song lilt to her voice, she said:

Now you are WIDE awake, Brad, yes? All clean and dry. I'm going to put you down right here next to our friend Ying-Ma, okay? [Brad smiles, gurgles contentedly, and flaps his arms up and down a couple of times as he settles on the carpet.] Yes, Lovey, I see you like that. Okay. I'll be back soon to play with you and Ying-Ma. Very soon.

Jesse then turned and walked quietly into the crib area. In some way that was unclear to me, she just seemed to know that Sanchi was in the process of waking up. To me, Sanchi was as quiet and motionless as she had been for the past hour or so. But, as Jesse moved closer to her, Sanchi shifted her body and turned her head in greeting, eyes wide open. Jesse responded in kind, "Hi, sweet girl. Did you have a good sleep?" Sanchi dropped the two fingers she had been sucking and answered with a smile. "Would you like me to pick you up now?" Jesse said, reaching both arms out in front of her, palms upturned. Sanchi lifted her arms toward Jesse. "Yes, I see you're ready. Here we go. Oh, you're getting to be such a big girl. Thank you for helping me!"

I jotted this note in my journal: "R-E-S-P-E-C-T, find out what it means . . . in this baby room!" (This was followed by a couple of little musical notes to remind me I was thinking about the Aretha Franklin song at that moment.) This guided me to focus my attention on the two co-lead care teachers, Jesse and Dylan, more closely and with a clearer purpose. Following their actions over the course of several days, I concluded that what seemed their "sixth sense" in terms of understanding their babies was a result of them knowing each of the babies so very well. They understood their rhythms, temperaments, likes and dislikes, and were able to read what to me seemed to be very subtle—or even nonexistent—cues. In my field journal, I labeled what I had seen as "the language of intimacy."

As I watched them, I concluded that most important of all was that their interactions with the babies showed genuine expressions of respect for them as individuals. It was amazing to watch Jesse and Dylan. Neither of these care teachers ever touched or moved or performed a caretaking action on a baby's body without asking for their assent. They waited patiently, until even the youngest babies gave some indication they understood and were okay with what the care teachers planned to do. The babies showed this with, for instance, eye gazes and smiles, kicking their legs happily, or with babbling and cooing sounds. Babies who were a little older indicated agreement or cooperation with large more controlled physical gestures such as raising their arms to be picked up or by repositioning their bodies to make whatever needed to be done a bit easier. These slightly older babies were also able to make their opposition to a request clear as well, shaking their heads, turning away, or even for some, saying, "No!"

There were many other important ways Jesse and Dylan engaged in communication with the babies. For instance, they both tended to narrate their way through the day, describing what they and the babies were experiencing. They emphasized certain words to make connections for language learning. "Look! The ball *rolled down* the slide!" said Dylan. "Feel how *cold* this snow is! *BRRR!*" exclaimed Jesse while making her body shiver. In quiet times on the carpet, or when feeding or diaper changing, I witnessed lovely moments in which these remarkably in-tune care teachers held conversations with babies. In such back-and-forth exchanges, they gazed into the eyes of the child, imitated their sounds and facial expressions, and often extended their speech attempts. "Babababababababa," said Kosuke, as he looked into Dylan's eyes. "Babababababababa," replied Dylan, adding "Babababa Baby! That's *you!* Bababa Baby Kosuke!" [Big smiles and laughs all around.]

Another important form of communication was demonstrated when the care teachers engaged babies in joint attention experiences, that is, "exchanging looks between an object and a partner solely to share attention about the object" (Schertz et al., 2017, p. 17). For example, when Jesse said, "Casey, do you see the pretty red bird at the bird-feeder?" she pointed to the bird feeder outside the window, looked at Casey, and then back at the bird-feeder. Casey pointed at the bird and cooed and wiggled excitedly in Jesse's arms. "Yes, you do see it. Oh, look at that! He just flew away. Bye-bye little red bird." They both waved bye bye.

So many of the communication events that I witnessed were lighthearted and fun—what I labeled "the language of joy" in my notes. In fact, much of the time in this baby room with co-lead care teachers Jesse and Dylan was filled with songs, rhymes, poetry, and laughter. Puppets and stuffed animals talked and sang in different voices, music played as everyone danced and moved and waved scarves. Even what might start as a quiet reading of a book with pairs or small groups of babies often ended with smiles, giggles, and signed requests for more. In fact, sign language—using simple words and phrases from American Sign Language (ASL)—was used frequently in this baby room. It was taught to babies and their families as an effective way of communicating with preverbal babies. The babies I observed seemed most familiar with the very useful signs for "more," "all done," and the universal sign of shaking their heads to say "No!"

As is inevitable in any group of very young children, there are moments of distress and sadness, of hurt, and occasional bouts of anger and jealousy. Dylan and Jesse excelled as communicators in these moments as well. They spoke quiet and calming words, always positioned themselves to be at the child's level, and provided eye contact and physical contact with a touch, a hug, or by picking them up and holding them close, depending upon what they knew comforted or calmed each individual baby most. These care teachers were never dismissive of a concern. Never was a baby told, "Oh, you're okay. Shhhhh" (which I hear far too frequently in childcare); but rather, they used phrases like: "I'll help you be okay," "Tell me what's wrong," "Can I help you?" and "I'm so sorry you feel upset (hurt, angry, and so on)."

There was one last important aspect of communication in this room that I found interesting, something I labeled in my notes as, "the language of consistency." In this baby room I witnessed the power of messages children received from the environment as a whole. The most vivid example of this came from my observations of 11-month-old Bo-Ji, who had arrived in the United States from China with his family just 2 weeks before I met him. In addition to that major life transition, this was Bo-Ji's first experience in childcare and hearing only English spoken.

Everything must have seemed so strange to him. No one looked or sounded like his parents, and his days were spent quite differently now than they had been during his life so far under his grandmother's full-time care. I tried to imagine how disorienting this must be, to see his world as it was for him now, so foreign. I was told though, that there had only been "a couple of rough days" when he first started. As I watched him now, he seemed perfectly content and engaged. In my field notes, I wrote, "How is Bo-Ji managing this so well?"

Bo-Ji was a happy and charming little guy. He was physically strong, and although not walking, he was a fast crawler, able to get around and pull himself up to a stand and cruise along furniture and play equipment very efficiently. He moved about the room engaging in multiple activities throughout the day and seemed interested and curious about what other babies were doing. After following his actions for a few days, I realized he was "reading" the room and the actions of the care teachers, especially Jesse and Dylan. After a couple of weeks of watching him, I concluded that the highly organized room and consistent routine were communicating to him. He had learned where to be and when, based upon what he could expect to happen.

Bo-Ji's observation skills allowed him to pick up on nonverbal cues provided by the care teachers about what would happen next and where he should go. Here are just a few or many examples:

- When Jesse put the soft round rug down on the floor in the gathering area, Bo-Ji would crawl over, ready to listen to her read or sing to them.
- As Dylan headed toward the cubbies and began gathering jackets and sweaters, Bo-Ji made his way over and presented himself to get ready to go outside.
- Soon after Ms. Cook, who delivered the lunch, came into the room and started washing her hands at the kitchen sink, Bo-Ji could be found standing at the lunch table next to his toddler-sized chair.

Bo-Ji had figured out how to "be" and to "belong" in this environment by paying attention to the cues communicated to him through the consistent routine and behaviors of his care teachers (Rutanen & Hännikäinen, 2017). The environment spoke to Bo-Ji! It reminded me of the often quoted idea that "the environment is the third teacher," attributed to Loris Malaguzzi of Reggio Emilia fame (Edwards et al., 2011). In this room, there certainly were three powerful care teachers, Jesse, Dylan, and the environment itself.

Reflection—The Right to Be Heard and Understood

Many readers will recognize that the title I chose for this story, "A Hundred Languages in Baby Rooms," is inspired by the famous book titled *The Hundred Languages of Children* (Edwards et al., 2011). This book is about a well-known approach to early care and education known as the Reggio Emilia Approach. Loris Malaguzzi, founder and inspirer of this educational philosophy wrote about young children having a hundred ways or more of expressing themselves—ways they listen and respond vocally and with their faces and bodies, how they show emotions as they play, sing, and dance, what they say about their artwork as they scribble and splash paint or neatly apply it, and in some many other ways. I love this way of thinking about language and how children communicate, so well expressed by Malaguzzi (n.d.) in his poem, "100 Languages" (as widely translated by Lella Gandini in Edwards et al., 2011). I identified just three languages (intimacy, joy, and consistency) in this composite story of my lived experiences in three different baby rooms, but there were so many more.

The idea of babies as communicators and as worthy communication partners is something I care deeply about and is the Big Idea in this story for me personally. Too often I encounter an underappreciation of the abilities of babies, especially in the area of communication. Even some of the undergraduate students who join the ECCE program at my university, at least at first, say they cannot see themselves working with children under the age of 3 years. They claim they would rather work with older children, arguing, "You can't talk to babies." Others complain, "They can't tell you what they need." "Oh, but they can, and they do!" I reply. Not only that, I add, "And we *must* listen to them."

According to Article 12 of the United Nations Convention on the Rights of the Child (2009), "it is every child's right to be heard" (Lansdown, 2011). This article asserts that being heard in terms of decisions that affect us is a matter of human dignity. Specifically, Article 12, number 1 reads: "States parties shall assure to the child who is capable of forming his or her own views the right to express those views freely in all matters affecting the child, the views of the child being given due weight in accordance with the age and maturity of the child" (United Nations, 2009, p. 3).

Personally, although I agree whole-heartily with the sentiment of that statement, I take some issue with the caveat about age and maturity. I believe *everyone, even* very young infants, is "capable of forming [their] own views." And thus, I also believe that *everyone* has the right to be listened to and taken seriously, at every age and developmental level. Yes, of course, there are decisions we must make as adults on behalf of children. But, just as Jesse and Dylan demonstrated, much, if not most, of the time it is feasible to honor the dignity of babies by communicating our intentions to them and providing them some choice in these matters whenever possible and safe.

Throughout this story, we see the respect shown by the care teachers for babies as both givers and receivers of information. I urge everyone to develop an appreciation of how children of all ages, including the very youngest, can and do express themselves. We must *all* open our eyes, ears, and hearts in order to see, hear, and feel what babies are saying to us and to respond appropriately.

Invitation for Further Reflection and Discussion

1. In this story, I identified three languages in my experience in this composite baby room: intimacy, joy, and consistency. What languages can you identify that are important in your own baby room or in the ones you have visited?

2. Clearly, the story speaks about communication, but do you see how the other key senses of well-being in this chapter, belonging and respect, are supported?

3. Think about your own style of communication with babies. Do you engage in conversations? Are they truly conversations, in that you engage in a back-and-forth informal chat, or would you describe your style as talking *to* more than talking *with* babies? (See Trevarthen, 2008; White et al., 2015.)

4. In notes I made when I experienced these events with Jesse and Dylan, I wrote, "It's like they're channeling Magda Gerber or Emmi Pikler!" What do you think I meant by that? (See Gerber & Johnson, 2002; Hammond, 2009; Solomon, 2013.)

5. How does your environment speak directly to the children in it? What does it say?

6. What do you think about the importance of regular expectations and routines in the environment and how they impact children, especially those new to the language or culture like Bo-Ji?

7. What are your thoughts about the Convention on the Rights of the Child's promotion of "children's voice" and the "right to be

heard and understood"? It makes some people uncomfortable because they believe by allowing children a direct say in what happens to them and what they want gives them too much power. How do you feel about this? Does the age or development of the child matter? If so, why, when, and how?

CLEVER BABY/BAD BABY

Preamble

In this story you meet Kara, a wonderful little 15-month-old bundle of charm and energy, at least that's how her morning care teacher saw her. Her afternoon care teacher had a very different view, one decidedly negative. How could the very same baby be seen so differently by her two key care teachers, the two people who, at least while she spent time in this baby room, knew her best? In the reflection following the story, I consider the Big Ideas of temperament and goodness of fit (Sravanti, 2017), and how they can impact a babies' experience of well-being in childcare.

Life Story

As I make the short morning drive to the childcare center where I'm conducting my research, I eye the sky with concern. Dark, swirling black clouds are rolling in quickly from the southwest, about to overtake the already gray October sky. This promises to be a thunderous and miserable day, I thought to myself, and I didn't mean just weather-wise, but quite possibly for Kara. Days stuck inside the Botanical Garden Baby Room, I had found, were Kara's hardest days. Or rather, I should say, *afternoons* without time to play outside were especially hard for Kara.

When I think of Kara, even to this day, I'm reminded of the children's poem by Henry Wadsworth Longfellow:

> There was a Little Girl
> And she had a little curl,
> Right in the middle of her forehead.
> When she was good
> She was very *very* good.
> But when she was naughty, she was Horrid!
>
> (Kramer, 1946, p. 289)

This story is essentially a story of *two* Karas, or rather two different ways this little girl was seen by her two key care teachers. Annie was the lead care teacher in the room, but each day after naptime, she left the room to work in her lab school office. The assistant care teacher Danielle, who was also there in the morning, stayed the rest of the day and took charge in the afternoon. A casual visitor in the morning may not even notice Kara as different in any way from the other busy, bustling crawlers, cruisers, and walkers playing in the room. If they did notice a difference, it might have been to find her just a little more physically active than some of the other babies. If that visitor came in the afternoon, however, they would likely witness a very different scene, one in which Kara played a starring role as she was chased and chastised, monitored and managed, and seemingly blamed for being, well . . . in my opinion, just for being herself.

Interestingly, there were many points of agreement between Annie and Danielle in terms of the words they used to describe Kara to me. They both used terms such as bright, energetic, fearless, easily distracted, opinionated, and fiercely independent. According to classic descriptions of temperament (Chess et al., 1963; Lally, 2011), Kara might have been labeled by some to be *difficult* or *feisty*. According to Allard and Hunter (n.d.), "A child's temperament describes the way in which she approaches and reacts to the world . . . her personal style" (para. 2).

Although the two key care teachers in this baby room agreed when it came to how they described Kara, Annie saw Kara in a positive light ("a joy") and Danielle as problematic ("nothing but trouble"). In truth, I found it harder to be with Kara in the afternoons. So much energy and attention seemed to be focused around controlling what she was doing, and there were often loud and long outbursts of her crying out in sadness, anger, or frustration. I jotted in my notes the question, "Why is Kara so difficult to handle in the afternoon?" I began to observe her more closely.

Was she sleeping well at naptime? Yes, she slept well. She was exhausted from the morning activities by the time the cots were placed on the floor, and she fell asleep as soon as her head hit her little pillow. Was she hungry? Not getting enough to eat? No, I concluded; she ate well. She was an eager eater who seemed to have a voracious appetite for anything put in front of her. So, the changes in her behaviors did not seem to be a matter of physical needs not being met. The physical environment itself was not any different from one part of the day to the next, and the morning and afternoon routines and activities mirrored one another closely. Adding to that, I quickly began to realize, except for a higher intensity of frustration in the afternoon, Kara's *actual* behaviors, the "ways" she engaged with the environment, were not discernibly different from morning to afternoon.

I slapped myself on my forehead and wrote, "Oh, *no*! I'm such an idiot!" I was horrified to realize that I had fallen into the trap of blaming the child. I am ashamed to admit that at least briefly, I had tried approaching this by looking at what was "wrong" with Kara. Of course, it was not Kara's fault! She was a 15-month-old baby girl! Trying to recover, I remember thinking about a phrase I often say to my undergraduate future teachers: "Children do not have to be ready for us; we have to be ready for each and every child who walks, crawls, or is carried into our rooms!" So, who was the "we" in this case? I began looking much more closely at the specific behaviors of Kara's care teachers as they related directly with her, during the morning and in the afternoon.

The constant person in Kara's day was Danielle, the assistant lead care teacher who was there both mornings and afternoons. Serena, a half-time assistant, arrived after naptime when Annie left the room. I quickly dismissed that Kara's rough afternoons could be related to Serena's interactions with her. They got along very well. And Serena, like her name would suggest, was calm, accepting, and loving to all the children, Kara included. In her own quiet way, she was also fun-loving and engaging, but she was simply not a "take charge" sort at all. Danielle, however, seemed to relish the role of being in authority in Annie's absence when she left after lunch. I began to see that "afternoon Danielle" was a different person in many ways from the one who worked side-by-side with lead care teacher Annie in the mornings. So although constant in her presence with Kara, she was inconsistent in her expectations for this little girl.

In the morning, Danielle always deferred to Annie. Annie herself was extremely patient and affirming of the children, and kind in her directions and redirections of the babies. She gently guided them away from danger or inappropriate behavior and helped them learn ways of being in this baby room and with their peers. An example of this comes to mind. One morning, Kara attempted to climb on top of one of the low toy shelves. Annie approached her, put an arm around her, and said, "Oh, Kara. You are such an *excellent* climber, but I'm going to pick you up, okay? [Annie picked her up and continued to speak to her face-to-face.] This is *not* safe. Please don't climb on the shelves. Would you like to climb on the climber, now? [Annie pointed to the climber.] Or you can wait and climb on the big hill when we go outside? Okay?" [Annie pointed out the window. Kara wiggles and squiggles, points to the climber, and practically jumps out of Annie's arms.] "That's my clever girl," Annie added as she placed Kara down near the ladder to the climber.

Asking Annie about this scene, and others similar, I said to her something like, "Kara sure is a handful, isn't she!?" "Oh, she's a delight," said Annie, "That's just Kara being Kara." Annie's acceptance of "Kara being Kara," was in remarkable contrast to Danielle's response when I made essentially the same comment to her one afternoon. "She knows what she's doing, and she acts that way on purpose just to get attention," Danielle told me, before adding, "She gets away with this kind of stuff in the morning, but not with me!"

As if to emphasize this point, later that afternoon I recorded the following episode. From across the room, Danielle noticed Kara knocking toys off the shelves of one of the toy storage units. She started to use the now empty shelves to climb up to the top. "KARA. Stop that NOW!" Danielle nearly shouted from across the room. As she walked briskly toward Kara, she added. "You are *not* going to do this! *No!*" Although not roughly, but certainly forcefully and abruptly, Danielle then picked Kara up and moved her a distance a few feet away from the shelves and sat her down on the carpet. "Look at this mess," Danielle mumbled as she turned her back on the now sobbing Kara and put the toys back, "where they belong." I added to my journal, "Hmm. They 'belong' but does Kara?"

I came away from my observations of Kara worried about what these differences in how adults saw her and responded to her might impact her sense of self, now and in the future. Did she think of herself as a clever little girl, ready to take on the world, or as a troublemaker who just never fit in? I worried about all the Karas I've known along the way and about how the match between them and the persons and environments they encountered impacted their social and emotional well-being.

Reflection—Temperament and Goodness of Fit

I think about Kara when I teach my future ECCE professionals about temperament and goodness of fit, the Big Ideas I consider in this reflection. The ways of looking at temperament have evolved over the years that I have been teaching, just as research about it has grown since Stella Chess and Alexander Thomas's work was widely published in the 1960s and 1970s. The broad labels of *easy, difficult,* and *slow-to-warm,* or some version of them, like *adaptable, feisty,* and *shy,* are still widely applied to children. And although we are always reminded, as Zero to Three (n.d.) asserted, "There is no right or wrong, better or worse temperament" (para 3), I find the labels limiting, and that they are too often applied in a judgmental or dismissive way.

When I teach about temperament, I urge students to avoid labeling children, but rather, to use temperamental characteristics to better understand how a child responds in various contexts and to different stimuli. Thomas, Chess, and Birch (1970) originally identified nine temperamental traits which many educators and parents find useful in sorting out the nature of a child's temperament "beyond the label." I personally find the five traits identified by Zero to Three (n.d.) to be more useful in understanding babies and their characteristic ways of interacting with people and the world around them; these are: emotional intensity and reactivity, activity level, sociability, coping with change, and frustration tolerance.

It is equally important to be fully aware of our own temperamental traits. This awareness helps us acknowledge any "hot buttons" we have that may trigger certain responses in a reactive, thoughtless way. Recognizing these within ourselves helps us learn to moderate our responses and to act as a counterbalance to children whose ways of responding we may otherwise find extreme. As adults, it is our responsibility to work toward a "goodness of fit" with all of the children with whom we spend our days (Kurcinka, 2006; Sravanti, 2017). In other words, we need to "fit" our responses and how we structure the environment and routines around a child in a good way—it is not the child's responsibility. This is not to say I believe anything goes. Of course not. One of our most important roles as care teachers is to promote social and emotional learning and development, including guiding children to learn to manage strong emotions and to act appropriately in social circumstances. As the Center for Parenting Education (n.d.) suggests, goodness of fit can help us choose our battles wisely, establish and maintain trusting and respectful relationships, and boost children's sense of feeling that they belong.

As I wrote this, I thought about one of my own personal "Karas" from my years as a care teacher, a wonderful ball of enthusiasm named Andy. As much as I loved Andy—and do to this day adore his adult self—I admit that I felt relieved on mornings when his mother would call to say he would not be coming in. The Karas and Andys we encounter can be difficult for many of us, without a doubt. Whether you are the kind of person who uses a great deal of energy to try to control such a child, or like me, you spend it trying to find a way to "fit" with them, you may end up exhausted at the end of the day. But my experience teaches me that it is well worth the effort. When met with compassion, the Karas and Andys of the world often grow up to be among the most interesting, talented, inquisitive, and passionate people you would ever want to have in your life.

Regardless, as professionals, it is important that we accept *all* children for who they are, while we provide guidance about how they can best *be* in the world and get along with others. To do so, it is important to look closely at each child's characteristic way of responding to the world. Awareness of the different ways that all human beings respond to stimuli around them helps us avoid problematic labels such as *difficult* or *slow-to-warm-up*. It helps us probe more deeply to address questions like: Why is she so bothered when I wrap her in this warm snuggly blanket? Why doesn't he like to play with finger paint? Why does she hesitate to join us and her friends in the sand box? And most important, what is best for this particular child? What does he need from me?

Invitation for Further Reflection and Discussion

1. This chapter is about belonging, respect, and communication. What do these senses of well-being have to do with this story

about Kara? How were they supported (or not) in this baby room?

2. Do you see yourself in this story? If so, who are you most like?
3. Were you a "Kara" as a child? Did you have trouble fitting in to the expectations of any of the adults in your life? How did this make you feel?
4. Is there a Kara in your life? Maybe many Karas? What are your concerns about them?
5. If you were Annie, the lead care teacher in this story and you found out what was happening with Kara in the afternoon, is there anything you would do about the situation? If so, what?
6. What is *your* temperament? Using the five primary characteristics of temperament (see Zero to Three, n.d.), how would you describe your characteristic way of interacting with the world? How do you feel when you encounter someone with very different temperament characteristics than your own? What if that person is a child?
7. How do you ensure a goodness of fit for *all* of the babies in your setting? Do you do anything to "fit" or adapt to the temperamental differences presented by the children with whom you work? Do you think this is important?

TEDDY "LEARNS" TO CARE

Preamble

In this story, I return to the Laboratory Greenhouse Baby Room featured in the story "Through the Looking Glass" in Chapter 2. As readers may recall, there was a great deal of crying in this room where the policy and practice required letting babies "cry it out." In "Teddy Learns to Care," I feature 12-month-old Teddy who experiences an unusual lesson from his care teacher about what it means to care for others. This is an expanded version of a vignette I used in an article, "Confronting the Baby Blues" about my time in that setting (McMullen, 2010). After the story, I reflect upon the Big Idea of how babies learn by observing those around them and from unintended messages we give them.

Life Story

I was halfway through my 2nd week of observations in the Laboratory Greenhouse Baby Room, and the tedious, robotic, and joyless nature of the daily routines were getting to me. Page after page of my observation notes showed I had recorded the same version of the same activity, over and over again, every 15 minutes of the day: "Kids moved to other play mat; new toys put out; position changed." The same thing happened every 15 minutes for nearly the whole day, every day. Every 15 minutes, the whole group of babies, whoever was awake at a given time, was moved first from one side of the room to the other. Both mobile and non-mobile babies were carried from the left side of this long, narrow rectangular room to the right, then from the right side to the left, and back again, and again, and again. Each time they were placed on first one squishy primary colored play mat and then its identical twin across the room.

The only real change during each rotation from one side of the room to the other was what toys and materials were dumped out from containers onto the play mat and in what body position the nonmobile babies were placed. In order to give them a "different perspective," I was told, and to "strengthen a variety of muscle groups," nonmobile babies' body positions were changed every 15 minutes—from their backs, to their fronts, from lying on one side to the other, and then placed into a piece of equipment that forced them to stand upright. Over and over and over again. When they moved the babies, the care teachers did not stop to see if the position seemed to be found to be comfortable or not, and they seemed to give no thought to whether a certain position might make more sense given the materials they were providing. Mobile babies were also expected to stay on the designated mat during each 15-minute cycle. (Note, there were no walking babies in this room, as walkers were moved to the next room with other toddlers as soon as they started walking.)

Despite this general tedium, one day I observed something I found particularly worrisome. This involved Teddy. Teddy was the oldest child in the baby room, a robust 12-month-old boy with unruly tufts of thick dark hair on his head. He was a competent and fast crawler, not quite walking yet. He was charming and sweet, and though he mostly looked quite serious, he rewarded me with big smiles whenever we made eye contact. So, of course, I tried to elicit that smile whenever I could! Watching Teddy and seeing him smile was one of the highlights of my time in that room.

The young undergraduate students who were Teddy's care teachers seemed in general to have their hands full with Teddy. He was not disruptive in any way, and as I said, he had a sweet nature. But the adult-oriented goals in this baby room and the care teachers' adherence to the routine were frequently at odds with what Teddy wanted to do. And, what he wanted to do—like most mobile babies—was to crawl about and explore the space and interact with the other babies! This was considered taboo, however, as one or more of the many care teachers always seemed to be chasing him down, to herd or carry him to where they wanted him to be.

And where care teachers wanted Teddy to be was on the designated play mat at the appropriate time. But also they very much wanted him to remain some distance away from the other babies. I found the care teachers hypervigilant when it came to Teddy. Their message was clear by their actions, "He is a brute who is going to hurt others." Honestly, I saw no evidence to support this fear. Whenever he crawled up to another baby, he approached them with curiosity and interest, not with any sign of aggression. As soon as he got close to another child though, it was as if an alarm had gone off. Someone would swoop in immediately, pick him up under the arms from behind to move him and say, "No, you play over here," or "leave [name of baby] alone, Teddy." When I asked about this, one of the care teachers said, "He's so big. He'll hurt someone." (Although robust and healthy looking, Teddy was a typically sized 12-month-old.) More than one care teacher expressed to me how eager they were for Teddy to start walking so he could be moved to the toddler room.

But as troublesome as I found these things, as I said, something happened one day that was truly confusing and worrisome. It was relatively quiet in the room. Most of the other babies were either being fed, having their diapers changed, or asleep in their cribs. There were just two babies left to participate for this particular 15-minute toy rotation, Teddy and Tammy. The care teacher had already removed the items from the plastic bin marked "baby care," and placed the toys on the empty mat. She then carried Teddy and Tammy, one at a time from the other play mat to begin this activity. As I wrote in McMullen (2010) from my field journal:

> It was the "Baby Care" toy rotation. The plastic bin has several baby dolls, plastic bottles, rattles, blankets, things to dress them up, etc. The contents of the bin lay in a pile on the play mat where the staff member sits cross-legged. Baby Tammy (4 months) is on her back right next to her, screaming bloody murder, literally inches away, completely ignored. Howling. Red-faced. Baby Teddy (12 months) is crawling around the mat contentedly. The staff member dutifully tries to engage him with that 15-minutes required toy selection. "Oh Teddy, look at the baby" (as she picks up a plastic baby doll from the pile of toys). "I think she's crying . . . wahhh wahhh wahhh. What do you think she needs?" Baby Teddy sits back on his bottom and looks at her. Staff rocks the plastic baby vigorously back and forth, talking gently and cooing to her. Meanwhile, the real Baby Tammy continues to scream. Staff makes fake "wahhh wahhh wahhh" crying noises again, pretending they are coming from the plastic baby. "Teddy, how can we help this poor baby? Should we try to wrap her in the blanket and give her a bottle? I wonder if she's hungry." The staff member wraps the [toy] baby up, and while Baby Teddy looks on, she rocks and feeds the bundled plastic baby, big, exaggerated rocking movements on her lap back and forth, singing her a song. Real Baby Tammy continues to scream on her back inches away from her. (pp. 8–9)

There was no sense of recognition from the care teacher as to the absurdity of what just happened. There was no discomfort or sense of irony displayed that what she showed Teddy about how to care for a crying doll baby was at complete odds with how she was treating crying baby Tammy. What a mess of messages about what it means to care for Teddy to muddle through and try to understand.

Reflection—Observational Learning and Unintended Messages

Reflecting on this experience, I was reminded of something my mother used to say to me, to my endless irritation and confusion as a child, "Do as I say, not as I do." Children who hear that phrase, Rymanowicz (2015) wrote, "will actually do both" (para. 1). In this case, it was my sincere hope that Teddy would do neither; that he would just ignore all of what he saw and heard in his lesson on how to care for babies. But is that a reasonable wish? We know from Bandura's (1977) development of social learning theory and his studies of *observational learning*, that children internalize what they experience and will repeat what they have seen and heard. This resulted in my reflecting on the Big Ideas of observational learning and the unintended messages that are communicated to babies.

Fagard et al. (2016) stressed how strong the influence of observational learning is, saying it "is probably one of the most powerful factors determining progress during child development" (para. 1). Children focus most attentively on the key persons in their lives who serve as models, passing on messages that can be negative, neutral, or positive. As Cherry (2021) emphasized, observational learning "plays an important role in the socialization process. Children learn how to behave and respond to others by observing how their parent(s) and/or caregivers interact with other people" (para. 4).

In addition to the confusing messages Teddy may have gotten from the episode of the baby-care activity, what concerns me is the possible impact on his developing sense of self and his relationships to others in this room and beyond. In this story, I describe how he was actively prevented from engaging with other children in the room. I think about the messages Teddy was probably getting about being "too big" and "too rough," and that he was someone who should be "kept away from other children."

But did the care teachers know they were saying this to Teddy? Was that their intention? I think not. The messages and the way they were being communicated to Teddy reminded me of what is talked about in various ways by different scholars as the "hidden," "implicit," or "accidental" curriculum. Jančec, Vorkapić, and Vodopivec (2019) described this in terms of "values, attitudes, norms, rules, and rituals" (p. 101) that a child learns in ways that were unplanned or unintended by the key adult model. For example, much of what we transmit to babies about our culture and how to live in our communities and societies is done in this manner (Costa & McMullen, 2020). And, of course, as we have learned and become much more sensitive to in recent years, implicit bias is also conveyed through the unintended messages from care teachers to young children, including babies. Not only can they do damage to the child to whom such messages are communicated, but there is danger that harmful biases about others will be internalized and transmitted by the children themselves. (See works by Walter Gilliam and colleagues from the Yale Child Study Center, such as Gilliam et al., 2016.)

Invitation for Further Reflection and Discussion

1. How does this story make you feel?
2. How does what happened in this story relate to the three senses of well-being that are the focus of this chapter—belonging, respect, and communication?
3. Describe what lesson about care you think Teddy may have learned from this experience. What might the babies in this room have learned about life, love, caring, and relationships?
4. I do not reveal whether Teddy's skin is white, brown, or black. In other words, I give no clue to his race or ethnicity. Would it matter in this story? Would it make a difference about how you interpret the way the care teachers kept him away from the other babies? Would it make a difference in how you feel about how they described his actions or potential to harm the other babies?
5. Are there care teachers with whom you work or have observed closely that are communicating hidden, and probably unintended, messages to babies that you think are strong, positive ones? How are they doing this? On the flip side, what are some of the messages you have seen conveyed, unintentionally, by other adults that you have tried to counterbalance or correct in some way?
6. Does my preferred title of "care teacher" for those engaged in the care and education of infants and toddlers seem appropriate for the adults in this baby room? If not, what would you call them? Caregivers, teachers, staff, professionals, or something else?

CONCLUSION

The life stories featured in this chapter speak to senses of well-being associated with belonging, respect, and communication. How do the three stories in the chapter underscore notions of acceptance and belonging, respect for personhood, being listened to and understood? Aspects of *belonging* in the stories illustrate how the characters do (or do not) feel connected to others in the baby rooms, and whether they experience the emotional climate as friendly and supportive. Ideas of *respect* are evidenced in what can be gleaned about how the babies and adults feel about themselves in terms of their self-worth and whether their family and culture is supported, accepted, and even celebrated in the environment. Finally, the stories show how the characters may feel they understand and are understood (or not), verbally and nonverbally, as well as whether they are listened to and responded to appropriately. The Big Ideas I considered as I reflected on these stories included the multiple ways of understanding and being understood in baby rooms, temperament and goodness of fit, and the power of observational learning and unintended messages.

CHAPTER 4

Engagement and Contribution

Imagine, for a moment, that you are in a work situation where you feel disengaged and that you have nothing of value to contribute. Put yourself in this scenario:

What you do all day, nearly everything you do every day, bores you to tears. When you awake in the morning, you are filled with a sense of dread about the tasks and people facing you when you arrive at work. The work you do goes largely unrecognized and seems unimportant to the people with whom you work or to the program as a whole.

Keep in mind, you are an adult who has choices. If the tedium and feelings that you not are needed, wanted, or valued grows too oppressive, you have a choice: Even if it would be difficult for you financially or otherwise, you could leave this position and try to find another. But what about children? Imagine what it is like for a baby in a space that provides no intellectual or physical stimulation, hour after hour, day after day, week after week.

A colleague of mine from England, Kathy Goouch, spoke to me once about how too many baby rooms are simply "parking" places for babies, not places to thrive. She emphasized that point, by showing an image of babies in strollers in parking spaces in a large parking lot. I have encountered others who speak of this as "warehousing," meaning babies are simply cleaned, fed, and kept safe from harm while their families are busy at work or school. But the parking or warehousing of babies does not support their well-being any more than it does the adults who share the space with them. All individuals, no matter what age, need to have opportunities to do things that are stimulating and interesting—fostering a sense of engagement. It is also important for an individual's well-being that the things they do matter, not just to that individual adult or baby themselves, but to others around them—fostering a sense of contribution. Thus engagement and contribution are essential elements of well-being.

UNDERSTANDING THE WELL-BEING SENSES OF ENGAGEMENT AND CONTRIBUTION

Of course, adults and children in baby rooms experience the senses of engagement and contribution through different activities and practices. The things that occupy our thinking, that we find interesting, and that bring us joy are different across the ages. The ways that we give back to those around us are different for the adult and the child. But like the other elements of well-being that I have described, the core of the lived experiences is pretty much the same in terms of how an adult or baby processes it both cognitively and emotionally. I describe these senses of well-being generally as follows:

> *Sense of Engagement* is experienced when an individual feels or knows that what they spend their time doing is enjoyable, personally meaningful, and intellectually and/or physically stimulating. These things they do may cause them to think differently in ways that challenge them but do not overwhelm them, or they may simply find them to be a very pleasant or even a joy-filled way to pass the time. Psychologist Martin Seligman (2011) said that for an individual to *flourish*, which he described as experiencing a state of well-being and happiness, humans need to live what he referred to throughout his

book as an "engaged life." Engagement, as he saw it, involves having things that interest us so much that we become absorbed in doing them to the point of getting "in flow" in which we use "the cognitive and emotional resources that make up thought and feeling" (p. 11). Some readers may be aware of psychologist Mihaly Csikszentmihalyi's (2008) very similar idea of flow that he considered necessary for an optimal experience in life. For some other readers, this way of thinking about engagement may call to mind Vietnamese Buddhist monk Thich Nhat Hanh's (1999) ideas about engagement that he referred to as the "miracle of mindfulness." *Mindfulness* is a state of being engaged so thoroughly in the moment, with full attention on what one is doing, to the point that little or nothing else distracts from that moment (McMullen & Dixon, 2009).

Sense of Contribution is experienced when an individual is entrusted with important tasks that recognize their strengths, capabilities, talents, and potential and in doing these things, the individual gives of themselves in some way to those around them, their group, family, or community. What they give can be something tangible, like providing help by performing a task that needs to be done or assisting someone who is struggling in some way (e.g., cleaning up after mealtime, helping a child solve a puzzle). Or the giving of oneself may be relatively intangible (e.g., affirming someone with a smile or nod, offering a supportive touch). Seligman (2011) believed that although an "engaged life" was highly important for one to flourish (i.e., experience well-being), engagement alone was deeply personal to the individual experience and thus in some way, selfish. Because of this, he asserted, engagement is not sufficient on its own for us to flourish; we must also have a "meaningful life." We achieve this by feeling that the things we do make valuable or needed contributions to those around us, including our families, communities, and societies.

Ideally, babies spend their days busily and happily engaged in activities and experiences that support their growth, development, and learning through play and active exploration, as well as through social interactions with others. They give back to us with smiles and laughs, cooperation as we perform tasks with them, and even by helping their peers and care teachers (e.g., handing a friend their pacifier or a toy, throwing away their lunch trash, positioning their bodies just so during diaper changing). This is their daily work in the baby room, and it requires that they expend energy, physically and intellectually.

Similarly, the engaged and contributing adult expends a great deal of energy each day in the baby room. This is not to say that all the work we do as care teachers is intellectually stimulating to the point of achieving flow as either Csikszentmihalyi (2008) or Seligman (2011) described it. Of course not. In fact, that work might go beyond stimulating to causing exhaustion. And though Hanh (1999) urged us to seek mindfulness even when doing mundane tasks such as washing dishes, few of us achieve mindfulness when wiping down a lunch table with bleach solution or sweeping the floor. But much of a care teacher's work *can* and *should* be engaged mindfully. This is especially true when what we are doing has anything to do with our direct interactions with babies, especially when it involves one-on-one interactions with them in routine care practices (e.g., diapering, feeding, helping them go to sleep) (Bussey & Hill, 2017). An intellectually engaged care teacher spends much of their time mindfully engaged in conversations and interactions with the babies and other adults; observing and assessing the environment and the children within it; planning ahead for the next moment, day, week, or even longer; and problem-solving in numerous big and small ways. Further the mindful care teacher refreshes and reinvigorates their mind by engaging in ongoing professional development throughout their career (Ackerman, 2006). And, yes, some of these things can even be done when wiping down tables or sweeping the floor.

The life stories in this chapter help us to think about how the well-being elements of engagement and contribution are achieved through productive and interesting work, play, and learning and our personal need to do things for the benefit of others. The two elements, working in tandem, involve both *structure* (policies, resources, infrastructure, and so on) and *process* (relational and interpersonal) aspects of care. As you read and reflect upon the stories, think about how engagement and contribution are present in each circumstance. Then consider how these elements are enhanced or diminished by the environments, relationships, and activities/practices in the baby rooms.

NEVER TOO LITTLE TO CARE

Preamble

Initially, my focus on the active and rambunctious group of mostly boys in the Wildflower Meadow Baby Room put me in danger of missing something and someone very special. But quiet and determined 11-month-old Faridah's actions and strong sense of right and wrong eventually captured my heart and my attention—and I'm so glad it did. It was because of Faridah that I learned just how fully capable very young children could be of kindness, caring, and even empathetic behavior. Faridah had given herself roles in the room as care teacher, nurturer, and fierce protector of the other children, especially when she believed the adults in the room were falling down on the job. For this story, I borrow excerpts from work I previously published with several infant/toddler care teachers in *Young*

Children in a piece titled, "Learning to Be Me, While Coming to Understand We" (McMullen et al., 2009). This story allowed me to reflect on the Big Idea of how we empower babies through child-centered scaffolding.

Life Story

On or about the 3rd or 4th day of my time in the Wildflower Meadow Baby Room, I realized that I was onto something special. Not only was this room turning out to be a fun place to be, but there was a spirit of caring for and about one another, between and among care teachers, babies, and family members that was uplifting and remarkable. I was seeing something that challenged me (in a good way) about my previous notions of prosocial learning and development and very young children acting in ways that demonstrate empathy. This realization left me shaking my head and eager to dig in and learn more.

As I focused my observations on the babies in this room (average age 10–11 months), I was privileged to witness many examples of prosocial behaviors being enacted by the babies (e.g., cooperation, affection, helping others). Care teacher Lucy described her beliefs about how early caring behaviors and acts of kindness emerge and are supported:

> I believe strongly that an infant's ability to be prosocial begins at birth and is continually fostered by the way the caregiver develops a loving, warm, and supportive relationship with the infant. Babies are delighted just to be with their friends and with their caregivers. [Lucy went on to provide an example.] When I was reading *Brown Bear, Brown Bear, What Do You See?* little Norah crawled right up close to me, pulled herself up, gave me a hug and made herself comfortable in the center of my lap. (McMullen et al., 2009, p. 24)

Although these types of behavior were prevalent in this room, one little girl really stood out to me. Faridah was a slightly built 11-month-old girl, quite new to walking, with stick-straight dark hair and unruly bangs. She wore a serious "I'm all business" expression on her face most of the time. And her business, it seemed, was to be a member of the care team alongside co-lead care teachers Vivian and Lucy, and their part-time aide, Ceylan. Faridah exhibited an extraordinary sense of awareness of others' needs, an awareness that went far beyond what I, at least until then, would have expected for someone so young. Could this be empathy? Isn't she too young?

I began to watch Faridah more closely. I found that it was common for her to pick up a forgotten pacifier found on the carpet and return it to the appropriate baby—she always knew whose it was! Likewise, she made sure that fallen sippy cups, bottles, or utensils at mealtimes were quickly retrieved and returned to their proper place or rightful owner. When a nose needed to be wiped, unbidden, Faridah would toddle over to the box of tissues, grab one or two and bring them to one of the nearest care teachers and insist that they deal with it.

But I wondered if the things that I saw Faridah do demonstrated that she was capable of empathy? In my mind at the time, empathy was a highly complex social–emotional skill that developed much later. It required not only the ability to see what someone else was seeing, in the way they were seeing it, but to also feel what they might be feeling. Someone who empathizes then acts to help that person, and that act is totally unselfish, to benefit the other. Was someone as young as Faridah able to do this? This conflicted with lessons I'd learned from long ago in graduate school about Piaget's insistence on young children as egocentric, in other words, unable to take the perspective of another (Piaget & Smith 2013.)

I knew firsthand from years of watching and studying young children and babies about the power of observational learning and what wonderful mimics they are (Bandura, 1977). I wondered if Faridah had seen someone in her family or one of the care teachers do things like this before, and she was simply imitating them. Maybe she found when she did these things, it pleased the adults around her, so she did them again and again. Was that all there was to it? "Well," I thought, "okay, maybe it is something like that." But I was still underestimating Faridah, convinced she was too young to be truly putting herself in the place of another and *knowing* or *feeling* what they might need. Then one day, while I was focusing on Faridah, I saw her do something quite surprising. Later, I asked her care teacher Vivian to describe it for an article written for *Young Children* (McMullen et al., 2009):

> Little Faridah seems to have appointed herself the "mommy police." We have a mom that comes at lunch to breastfeed her infant son, and sometimes he falls asleep just before she arrives. Faridah often sits and plays near his crib, waiting for him to wake up, keeping her eye on him. If, while waiting, the mom picks up another baby, Faridah gestures at the crib and the mom, and squeals with a tone that indicates she is correcting the parent. (p. 25)

It was now that I began to believe Faridah's actions indicated she was capable of empathy. I wrote in my journal that this was my "last straw" when it came to my earlier and naive wholesale adoption of Piaget's stage theory (which had admittedly been unraveling for me for years). Faridah was clearly acting voluntarily and in ways that seemed intentionally meant to benefit someone else. She was not reenacting something she had seen her care teachers do in this room. Vivian, Lucy, and Ceylan certainly did not chastise mothers for paying attention to babies that were not their own.

More evidence that this was empathy was that the care teachers and I, together, witnessed this event the first time it happened, so it was not a repeated behavior that had been positively reinforced. I reminded myself how it is always dangerous and a sign of arrogance (and a bit of egocentrism on my own part) to think, as an adult, that I really could know what is behind a child's thoughts, feelings, and subsequent actions. But those of us who saw this, all interpreted it the same way—as an indication that Faridah felt the mother was behaving inappropriately and that somehow, her sleeping friend's rights or feelings were being violated.

There were other observations of Faridah's behavior that I recorded and noted as "empathy" in the margins of my journal. One in particular stands out. It happened outside on the playground. As with any group of children this age, most of them were doing their own thing. The eight babies were scattered about, mostly on the grass under the big tree, sitting or on their tummies playing quietly with toys or seeming to simply enjoy the sunny, breezy day. All were under the watchful eyes of the care teachers. Two of the babies, both competent crawlers and cruisers, caught my attention. They were both trying to climb into a big old giant truck tire embedded in the sand. One, Ceci, upon reaching her goal of getting inside the tire, picked up a plastic toy sand shovel she'd found and stood up along the rim of the tire rather triumphantly. The second baby, a little boy named Tory, tried to grab it and wrestle it away from Ceci who was holding on tight. "Nooooo!" cried Ceci, lower lip quivering with righteous rage and indignation. Like a shot, Faridah was in the picture. She positioned herself right next to Ceci where they stood shoulder to shoulder. Staring straight into Tory's eyes, she shouted, "Noo! Noooo! Nooooooo!" Seemingly stunned, Tory the would-be shovel thief, sat back down in the sand and crawled off.

I turned to Lucy who stood next to me. "Wow! She is powerful," I said. Lucy responded with laughter and added, "Yeah, and it's a good thing she uses her power for good instead of evil."

Reflection—Prosocial Behaviors of Babies in Baby Rooms

My title for this story, "Never Too Little to Care," emerged from a place of wanting to find hope for the future. The last couple of years have left me needing to refill my glass to at least half full again. Pandemic, political tensions, long unaddressed racial injustices, the rising distrust of science, and the prevalence of "fake news" and conspiratorial thinking had drained me dry. As I relived my time in the Wildflower Meadow Baby Room and wrote down the story of Faridah, I began to envision a way forward with and through our children and by helping them realize their own innate capacity for caring and kindness to themselves and others (Paulus, 2014). It is never too soon. I believe that in baby rooms, we do this by modeling caring and kind expressions and behaviors and by reinforcing prosocial behaviors as they emerge in and are practiced by our babies. This Big Idea is important, not only for the children as individuals but to the well-being of society itself (Eisenberg et al., 2015).

Frankly, as indicated in the story, I must admit to my own surprise at how early prosocial behaviors and the ability to empathize with others emerge. At the time, to process and understand what I was seeing, I had to dig into the published research. Thinking back, I had always assumed that the nature of babies from birth is to be social—everything I knew from learning about child development, attachment theory, and from my own three babies taught me that. But I had clearly underestimated how early babies were capable of engaging in outward expressions of care such as helping, sharing, comforting, and showing concern toward others. The research had exploded with new findings around this topic since I had been in graduate school. This experience was a reminder to me to keep up with the research and to continue to educate myself.

Trevarthen and Aitken (2001) confirmed what had been my existing beliefs about social behaviors beginning at birth, with even our youngest newborns seeking ways to engage with others. Other researchers have confirmed that prosocial acts begin as early as the first year of life (Davidov et al., 2013). Liddle, Bradley, and McGrath (2015) found babies as young as 8 months attend to and express distress when their peers are upset. This was confirmed by Köster's research team (2016) which found that babies as young as 9 months can understand another's needs. What had originally been dismissed as "contagious crying," where one baby cries, then another, is now reframed by many scholars as early prosocial behavior. The chorus of crying that occurs in our baby rooms (something most of us have experienced) is not simply like wolves calling to one another across a distance. Rather, it is now thought to be recognition that someone else is in distress (Geangu et al., 2010). Finally, and I think amazingly, we also now know that babies have certain expectations of the adults around them to be helpful when someone needs them. Jin et al. (2018) found that babies expect adults to comfort other babies when they are distressed.

Although empathy—that ability to know, understand, and feel what others are feeling—is a prosocial behavior, it is certainly a very complex form of being prosocial. Theoretically, it requires a child to know they are individuals who are separate and apart from other people, and even more complicated, that those individuals have thoughts and perspectives that may be different from their own. Quann and Wien (2006) defined *empathy* in young children as "the capacity to observe the feelings of another and to respond with care and concern for that other" (para. 4).

This says nothing about their capacity to *feel* what the other feels, nor what their motivations are. Is it to help the other child, or is it done to please the adults around them? Does it matter?

I'm not sure it does. The question is, was Faridah imagining how the *other children* might be feeling or did she envision how *she herself* would feel in that same situation? It is a subtle distinction, and it may not be important, but it is something those who debate about the origins of true empathy may wish to consider. Either way, what I saw in Faridah fits Eisenberg's (1992) definition of *empathy* in very young children, "voluntary behavior intended to benefit another, such as helping, sharing, and comforting" (p.3), and thus is important to encourage in baby rooms and beyond.

But not all of the babies we may meet in baby rooms will demonstrate empathy and prosocial behaviors as vividly as Faridah did in this story. Many of them will, however, engage in acts of kindness that I believe should not be ignored. In McMullen et al. (2009), we defined *prosocial behavior* for babies in group settings as

> the communications and behaviors on the part of a baby that help create a positive emotional climate in the group and that involve reaching out— positive, discernable, outward social expression on the part of one baby toward one or more other individuals, whether infant or adult. (p. 21)

Such behaviors should be encouraged in babies to increase their likelihood of being repeated. We now know prosocial behaviors emerge early and increase as children grow and develop. We also know engaging in and experiencing these behaviors is essential for young children's social and emotional development while they are still babies, and as they form social relationships throughout life (Eisenberg et al., 2015).

Prosocial behaviors and early empathy are thought also to be outward signs of moral development (Eisenberg et al., 2006; Knafo et al., 2008; Liddle et al., 2015). Faridah certainly seemed to take it as a moral violation when her friend's mother attended to a baby that was not her own. Hamlin (2013) spoke of such things as evidence of "an innate moral core" in human beings that "evolved to sustain collective action and cooperation as required for successful group living" (p. 186). Helping our youngest citizens develop morally and prosocially is, to me, one of the most important contributions a care teacher can make, not only to the child, or to the group in the baby room, but to society as a whole.

Invitation for Further Reflection and Discussion

1. In what way is this story about prosocial behavior and empathy related to the well-being senses of engagement and contribution?

In your response, consider both care teachers and the babies. How does this form of engagement and contribution, potentially, impact families and society as a whole?

2. Discuss some of the ways in which you have seen early prosocial or empathy in very young children. How did you or the other adults respond when you witnessed it? Did you say something to the child? (See Lerner & Parlakian, n.d.) Of course, we also deal with antisocial behavior from time to time. What is your response at these times?

3. Do you think that being in group childcare makes a difference in how early prosocial behavior and empathy might emerge in a child? In other words, is it the same or different for the baby who is at home without other babies or young children around them? How might it be different?

4. Do you see the emergence of prosocial behavior as related somehow to moral development? If so, how? What is moral development in very young children? (See, for example, Parlakian, 2017.) Some people find the idea of having a role in the moral development of the babies in their care makes them uncomfortable. Why do you think this might be? How do you feel about it?

THE BABY FIX

Preamble

This is a composite story in which I share something I experienced several times in the Meditation Garden and the Wildflower Meadow Baby Rooms. Here, I feature co-lead teachers Sue and Dan and assistant Cary as stand-ins for all those individuals I saw endure this rather strange phenomenon that I call, "The Baby Fix." I describe how throughout the day, professional colleagues from the toddlers, twos, and preschool rooms in this composite childcare program flowed in and out of the baby room, staying only a few minutes at a time. Were they there to help? Who benefited from their visits? We also meet the director of the program, Ellen, who enters the room and engages with the individuals in it in a very different manner and with a different purpose than so many others. In the reflection, I consider the Big Idea of the importance of respecting the work and play in baby rooms.

Life Story

From where I sat, cross-legged on the floor in the corner, I saw the care teachers and children busily occupied throughout the baby room. Near the book display shelf, I spotted Sue reading quietly but animatedly on the floor with three babies. They were snuggled up close to one another, all eyes fixed on the *Goodnight Moon* bunny. I looked over at Dan, grinning to myself at the image of this very tall man sitting on an impossibly small chair in front of two short highchairs. I watched as he spoon-fed two little guys what looked like mushy squash, and my grin widened as I saw them respond with messy-faced smiles to something Dan was saying. My attention was then grabbed by giggles coming from over by the big windows. Here, Cary was captivating the attention of a small group of three babies who swatted gleefully at the bubbles he blew. From my vantage point, sunlight reflected off the bubbles, resulting in a rainbow of colors. "Ahh, I just love it here," I thought to myself.

And then, at that moment, when everyone seemed busily and contentedly engaged in the things they were doing, the hall door to the baby room burst open. "Give me some *love!*" The woman at the door nearly shouted. As the door shut noisily behind her, she flung her arms wide, and said, even more loudly than before, "Geena's here! *Babies, Geena is here!*" The woman then moved with purpose into the room and sat on top of a toy shelf. She slapped her thighs three times with her hands and said, "Come and give me some *love!*"

Although all eyes and all attention were now on Geena, one little guy, Mikey, was particularly attracted to her call. He left behind his snugly space next to Sue and her book reading, crawled quickly over to Geena, and reached out his hands to be picked up. She picked Mikey up, and then practically gushing, she said, "*Yes,* you do *love* Geena, don't you!" While still seated on the bookshelf, she held Mikey on her knees, his legs over hers facing toward her, her hands cupped around his. She continued. "And Geena loves *you!*" Geena then called over to Sue, several feet away. "Did you hear about what happened to . . ." Without waiting for a response from Sue, Geena proceeded to tell her a rather long-winded story about something that had happened with a colleague down the hall. With dramatic flair and sweeping gestures, she shared what sounded to me to be gossip about a topic quite inappropriate for very young children to hear. She moved Mikey's arms up and down, in and out and away from his body like he was some kind of prop in the telling of her tale. All the while, Geena looked into Mikey's eyes as if she was talking just to him, and he responded with delighted laughs and a big smile to her sing-songy tone. Sue was polite to Geena, but just. Her body language told me she was annoyed.

Then, almost as suddenly as she arrived, and after what had amounted to no more than 5 minutes, Geena announced it was time for her to return to work. She put Mikey down on the carpet at her feet, got up, and headed toward the door. Mikey looked alarmed and confused and started crawling after her. "I have to go now, babies. Remember, Geena *loves* you!" Then, as if performing for an audience, she threw kisses to all corners of the room. "I'll see you later!" Mikey stopped crawling, sat back on his knees, looked up to Geena's face and using sign language, he made the sign for "more." "Oh, look at that!" laughed Geena loudly. "He wants 'more.' *More Geena!*" She clapped her hands and was laughing as she shut the door behind her. Mikey laid down on the floor, sobbing wretchedly.

Sue got up from the carpet, leaving two babies and the unfinished book behind. She picked Mikey up and, holding him close, she rocked him slowly in her arms. I came to her and asked, "What was that?" "That," she said, "was Geena. And Geena happens nearly every day." Sue went on to inform me that the results of Geena's visits were nearly always the same. For whatever reason, Mikey was very attracted to her, and when she leaves, he cries for several minutes. "And she's not the only one," added Sue. Apparently, staff members from other rooms occasionally dropped by for a few minutes during their breaks. Sue said the others were usually not nearly as disruptive as Geena, and that, "they are sometimes actually helpful, except when all they want to do is chat." It took about 20 minutes for activity and emotions to return to pre-Geena levels that day and on each and every day that I witnessed Geena's performances.

I scribbled in my notes about how I found Geena's behavior "disrespectful." Geena had interrupted something very special that was going on in the room. Even if Geena was on break, Sue, Dan, and Cary were not—they were fully engaged, working *with* the babies. And the babies themselves were fully engaged with what they were doing—reading with Sue, having a nice conversation with Dan while eating lunch, or experiencing the wondrous bubbles being blown by Cary. Why did Geena assume they were available to drop everything and chat with her to pass the time? Such behavior disregarded the important work and play of the adults and the children in the baby room. And it was certainly disrespectful of Mikey. I wrote the following not very kind note about Geena: "She's using Mikey to boost her own ego. She seems to wear it as a badge of honor that he sobs every day when she leaves."

I began to follow this phenomenon more closely in my remaining weeks of observations. Geena continued to visit most days, and each time was much the same as the one I first experienced. Granted, no other drop-in visitors were as loud and flamboyant as Geena—not by a longshot—but nearly all of the unexpected visitors interrupted activity in some way. I don't believe any of the drop-ins were intentionally disruptive. Of course not. I think they probably would have said (and probably believed) that they were coming into the baby room to help. Passing a few minutes of break time by chatting with friendly colleagues and holding and rocking babies was a very pleasant and even a calming way to relax before returning to their own busy childcare rooms. "I gotta get me some shugga," one of them was fond of saying, before sometimes dozing off in the sliding rocker with a baby held to her chest. This is when I started referring to the fly-by visits as "the baby-fix" in my observation journal.

Clearly, these visitors were *getting something out of* the babies and care teachers when they dropped in, and just as clearly (for the most part), babies and care teachers did not benefit equally. But sometimes they did; there were times when colleagues entered the room when they knew it would be a busy time, or when from outside the room they could hear things were getting a bit chaotic. We've all experienced those moments when everyone seems to be in need of something at the same time, they are very insistent about it, and there just doesn't seem to be enough hands on deck! Ellen, the director of the program, notably and reliably, was one of those people who always seemed to arrive at just the right moment.

The same day that I had my first encounter with Geena, Ellen also visited. It felt like it was just about to become one of those chaotic moments. I could just feel it, like everyone was going to need some attention. I hardly noticed when Ellen arrived, she was so quiet. I saw her at the door as she glanced around quickly to take in what she was seeing. Turning, she closed the door softly behind her, walked in with slippered feet, and headed straight over to Sue who was giving a baby a bottle in the sliding rocker, with another child clinging to her leg and sniffling in a fretful manner. Bending over, and speaking softly into Sue's ear, she asked, "What do you need me to do?" Sue looked up with gratitude in her eyes, "Oh, thank you, Ellen. I'm so glad you're here. Mikey needs to be changed, and Gabrielle is ready for a snuggle and a nap. Do you mind?" "Of course not," responded Ellen, immediately, "I'm here to help."

Reflection—Respecting Work and Play in Baby Rooms

When I reflect on this story, the Big Idea for me centers on respect. It is about respect for the important work and play of the adult care teachers and the babies in the room. Or, unfortunately, this story is more about the *lack of* respect, however unintentional, that was shown to children and the care teachers in the baby room by their own colleagues.

At the time that I experienced this, and still to this day as I write this story, I like to imagine a 10th-grade geometry teacher standing at the white board in front of her classroom. She is showing the class how to write a particularly difficult mathematical proof. Halfway through class, in saunters one of her colleagues who happens to have a free period from teaching. He carries coffee and a newspaper, sits in a nearby chair and puts his feet up on one of the empty desks. As he flips through the pages, he says, "Hey, Sheila (the math teacher), did you see this? Barry (their chemistry teacher colleague) got arrested for drunk driving."

That example is extreme and perhaps seems a bit absurd. This would be disruptive and inappropriate for one high school teacher colleague to do to another. It would be interrupting the important work of teaching and learning. But, even if we consider something closer to the reality of this story, it still seems inconceivable to me that one's colleagues could be so thoughtless. Imagine for a moment that Geena was in the middle of circle time with her group of 3- to 5-year-olds. Maybe she is talking with them about an incident in which one of the children's feelings were hurt, or perhaps she is in the middle of reading a story, or maybe one of the children is telling about his visit to his grandparents on the weekend. In walks Sue from the baby room. "*Hellllllooo kids!*" she practically roars. She proceeds to take a preschooler out of the circle and hold him in her lap. She then tries to engage Geena in conversation.

These things just do not happen, do they? Not in the 10th-grade math classroom or the preschool room. So why is it something I have witnessed so frequently in baby rooms? Is the work and play going on in these rooms any less important than the work of the adults and children in preschool rooms? This is just one of the ways that people, even well-meaning colleagues, are dismissive of what happens in baby rooms. I really struggle when I witness, read, or hear about how infant/toddler care teachers are underappreciated and how in big, small, and usually unintentional ways, they are disrespected by others. In part, it is because I experienced this firsthand when I was an infant care teacher at the beginning of my career. "When are you going to graduate out of this room and do something interesting," I was asked by one of my colleagues who worked with 4- and 5-year-olds in the same program.

Kathy Goouch and Sacha Powell (2013), colleagues of mine from England, spent over a decade studying and supporting the professionals who work in baby rooms in their country. The care teachers whom they studied spoke of many issues that impacted how they saw themselves as professionals. Chief among them, as it would probably be in the United States, were low wages and few if any benefits. But also prevalent were complaints about what they experienced as a lack of recognition and the devaluing of their work by colleagues, administrators, some of the families of the children in the room, and society as a whole.

Many of us in early childhood at almost any level have experienced some form of this as well, from baby rooms to university classrooms. ECCE professionals struggle to be seen as more than baby-sitters, and as a college professor, I have struggled throughout my career to make other scholars understand the importance of studying young children, and in particular, children under age 3. I was asked once by one of my university colleagues, "What's a smart woman like you doing studying babies?"!

Invitation for Further Reflection and Discussion

1. I begin where I ended my personal reflection by asking, more generally: What are smart people like us doing working with babies (e.g., as care teachers, administrators, researchers, and policymakers)? How would you respond if asked this question?
2. What do the behaviors described in this story have to do with engagement and contribution?
3. Have you ever experienced having colleagues come and spend time, at their convenience, in your baby room? How did you feel about it? If you have not experienced this, how do you think you would feel?
4. Have you ever been the "I gotta get me some shugga" kind of pop-in visitor to a room, just needing your baby fix? Do you see yourself as one of the other characters in this story? Who? Have you ever been the Geena in this story, or even a milder version of her? Or do you picture yourself more like Ellen?
5. Perhaps you welcome the brief interludes when others visit your baby room unexpectedly. In what way do you like it? Have you ever thought about how this behavior could be distracting and maybe even annoying for those in the room, your care team partners or the babies?
6. If you do find this problematic, what do you think might be the best way to discourage this kind of behavior from your colleagues? Put them to work? Ask them politely not to do this? Complain to the director?
7. Did you notice there were two male care teachers in this baby room—Dan and Cary? That is unusual, at least in the United States, where men are still a very small minority of the workforce in ECCE settings. What are your feelings about this? For instance, do you wish more men were involved? Why or why not? Does the age of the children with male care teachers matter to you?

TRAINING STARFISH BABIES TO "PLAY"

Preamble

In this story, I am continuing my observation of the Laboratory Greenhouse Baby Room. Here I detail what I experienced when I observed care teachers remaining faithful to a rigidly prescribed curriculum and practices without considering the needs, interests, and developmental capabilities of the children. As I did in the story about Teddy in Chapter 3,

I draw on material previously shared as a short vignette in my article "Confronting the Baby Blues" (McMullen, 2010). In the life story and the reflection that follows it, the Big Idea that I focus on is what we can do to encourage meaningful play in baby rooms and the need to select materials with which children can fully engage.

Life Story

Sometime during my second week of conducting research in the Laboratory Greenhouse Baby Room, I decided to focus on *play* and what it meant in this room. I had already concluded—probably my 1st day there—that my notions of play as something child-driven, personally meaningful, and enjoyable did not describe what was happening here. Play in this room was far from joyful, and sadly, what the care teachers referred to as "playtime" occupied most of the day. Puzzling this out was not going to be easy, and I knew it. It was like I was in an upside-down world. Here, often, the adults were the ones playing with the materials while the babies watched or looked away disinterested. Furthermore, most of the materials were designed for children who were at least 2 or 3 years old, not children under the age of 1, as were all the babies in this room.

By this time in my stay in this room I had also learned that in addition to there being no choice-making for children about anything they did during the day or the materials they could play with, the care teachers similarly lacked choices. Schedules defined what toys were to be put out at any given time and care teachers tried admirably to interest babies in the materials, as they had been instructed to do. Encouraging the babies to engage with the toys was a mostly hopeless gesture, I observed, for several reasons. First, most of the toys held little or no interest for the babies. (Just imagine, for instance, trying to engage a group of babies under the age of 1 with the contents of a doctor's kit.) Second, even if certain materials did grab their interest, the babies were seldom given an opportunity to simply explore them on their own without adults showing them "how to do it." And, finally, because the babies were constantly being moved from one toy experience to another throughout the day, they had little time to develop an interest in any given item.

The toys were stored as sorted into playsets (e.g., plastic toy rotary telephones, cloth puppets, plastic animal models, toy dishware). Dozens of these playsets were then stored in transparent plastic boxes with lids, with their labels facing out. The boxes lined four unsteady looking wooden-plank shelves held up with metal clips that ran the 12-foot length of one long wall of the baby room and reached nearly to the top of the eight-foot ceiling. All toys were out of reach of the children until the designated box was made available to them during the appropriate toy rotation period. Figure 4.1 shows the laminated toy schedule posted on the wall that day that designated what playset to use at what time.

During each 15-minute toy rotation, a different set of toys was placed on one of two soft play mats on the floor. Then all the babies, mobile and nonmobile, were moved to that mat to play. One particular toy rotation that caught my attention this day involved five nonmobile babies plus a little girl named Sun-Mi who had just begun pulling herself along on her belly commando style.

At 11:00 that morning it was Waffle Block Time. Small waffle blocks colored bright red, yellow, green, and blue were dumped in a pile in the exact middle of the bright, primary-colored mat. "Well, that's confusing," I wrote, "You can barely see them!" Some of the blocks were fashioned together to form cubes, others remained as separate, individual pieces. I watched as a care teacher carried the five nonmobile babies, one at a time, from the mat where they had "played" with puppets from 10:45 to 11:00 to this second mat. She placed these babies on their backs in an array, with their toes facing inward toward the middle of the mat (and the toys), and their heads positioned at points the furthest away from the center. "OMG!" I wrote, "They look like a starfish."

Leaving the starfish babies to "play" with the waffle blocks (none of which were within their reach), the care teacher retrieved Sun-Mi and placed her on the carpet alongside the starfish babies' mat. Taking the two

Figure 4.1. Sample of a Daily Play Schedule

Wednesday Play Schedule

8:00	TRANSPORTATION	12:45	ANIMALS
8:15	ANIMALS	1:00	BALLS
8:30	MEGA BLOCKS	1:15	RINGSTACKERS
8:45	PHONES	1:30	RATTLES
9:00	SOFT BLOCKS	2:00	BOOKS
9:15	TOOLS	2:15	FOOD
9:30	BOOKS	2:30	MIRRORS
10:00	SHAPES & SORTERS	2:45	BABY CARE
10:15	FOOD	3:00	PEOPLE
10:30	STACKING CUPS	3:15	STAR BUILDERS
10:45	PUPPETS	3:30	MUSIC
11:00	WAFFLE BLOCKS	3:45	BEAN BAGS
11:15	PEOPLE	4:00	DOCTOR KITS
11:30	MUSIC	4:15	SEE & SAYS
11:45	DISHES	4:30	POP BEADS
12:00	DRESS UP	4:45	DISHES
12:15	PLASTIC BLOCKS	5:00	RING STACKERS
12:30	SCARVES	5:15	BRISTLE BLOCKS

sets of waffle blocks that were stuck together to form cubes from the center of the mat, she proceeded to demonstrate and then urge Sun-Mi to stack them, one on top of the other. Eventually, the care teacher cupped her hand around Sun-Mi's and then moved her hand and an arm, so that together, they stacked the blocks. "Good job, Sun-Mi! You stacked two blocks!" They then practiced it over and over five or six more times, always with Sun-Mi's arm and hand being supported to complete the task. At no time did Sun-Mi seem the least bit interested in what they were doing.

This was certainly like nothing I had ever seen before, and no, I concluded, I did not like it, not one bit. But it made me think seriously about how to defend my beliefs about play and development at this age as something that is meant to unfold and be supported through sensorimotor discovery and exploration, not forced through repetitive training exercises. Although in past observations of children experiencing developmental delays of one type or another, I had witnessed such highly controlled adult (teacher or therapist) planned activities, it never occurred to me that this would be done with children who had no identifiable special need.

I turned my attention to considering the purpose of these training sessions. In a weird (backwards world) way, some might say the objectives were "developmentally appropriate" because they were individually designed for each baby. (But that's where any resemblance to developmentally appropriate practice ends.) The goals for each baby, by name, were hung on the walls around the room to remind care teachers what to work on during "play." "Roll stomach to back; pull to stand; stack 2 objects; lift head to 45-degree angle; shake and bang objects together for 5 seconds; and so on," depending upon the baby. These adults, all young undergraduate college students, were required to teach and coach children to achieve these goals, as I described in the following excerpt from McMullen (2010):

> Staff members worked on the goals with individual babies during scheduled play times, moving them into position, cajoling them, pleading with them, speaking to them in loud sing-song voices, gesturing, ordering them, and sometimes doing the tasks for them. If a baby accomplished the desired behavior on his or her own, the staff member would first verbally praise the child and then shout out to another adult in the room, for example, "Tammy pulled to hands and knees at 9:43 a.m. Record it." Babies who accomplished a goal with assistance were also praised: "Good rolling, Tammy. That's the way to roll!" (p. 5)

The care teachers in this baby room were clearly proud of what they thought they had accomplished with the babies. One afternoon, I watched as a baby pulled himself to a standing position, holding onto one of the unsafe looking shelves holding the plastic toy sets. "Look!" said his big brother who had just arrived with the baby's mother to pick him up to go home. "He's standing up!" One of the care teachers jumped in, beaming, "I taught him that," she said. "OMG," I wrote in my field journal as I recorded this incident, "they really think they are *teaching* these babies to reach normal developmental milestones."

Reflection—Encouraging Meaningful Play in Baby Rooms

At the beginning of this chapter, I spoke of parking or warehousing of babies in group care—the practice of simply making sure they are clean, fed, and remain safe while their families are away during the day. But as I reflect on this story of the starfish babies, I wonder if the type of engagement babies experienced in the Laboratory Greenhouse Baby Room was better or worse than if they had simply "parked" for the day. In one of my ECCE courses, I have the students unpack the following ideas about engaging babies in childcare: "You can do *too much for* a baby"; "You can do *too much to* a baby"; and "You can do *too little with* a baby." I see parking or warehousing, as one example of doing "too little with," whereas I believe this story represents how the care teachers did "too much to" the babies in this room.

The Big Ideas for me from this story involve play, specifically, what it means in this baby room and how playtime is used to try to influence the babies' development. Of course, the nature and reasons for play differ somewhat across cultures and countries. But it nearly always includes some common elements. For example, play for babies and children is generally thought to be something enjoyable or fun. And many or perhaps most of us reading this believe play should be mostly or completely child-led and allow for some degree of freedom of choice in terms of the materials or activities in which children can engage during playtime. However, standing in stark contrast, play in the Laboratory Greenhouse Baby Room was generally joyless, it was always adult-directed, and the babies had no choice of what toys and materials they could use. Thus, in my opinion, play in this baby room was meaningless *for the babies*, at least as I and many others might see it.

But playtime in this room *did* have meaning and purpose to those who ran the program and the adults within it. Playtime allowed opportunities for the training and coaching of babies to reach the next developmental milestone. I expressed my views on this in a recent book (McMullen & Brody, 2021) where my coauthor, an infant/toddler care teacher, and I wrote:

> Although you may be able to hurry along the achievement of some developmental milestones, when tempted to do so, please ask yourself, "Why rush?"

Although training a child to crawl, walk, or say "mama" might result in that child beating their own internal clock by a few days or a couple of weeks, why does it matter? Is it for the child's benefit? Did they enjoy the process? Rather, we urge you to provide environments, experiences, and play materials that support development as it unfolds in the individual children in your settings. (p. 14)

Rather than training babies and using toys simply as a means to an end, most of us in this field advocate supporting children's development by allowing them to engage with materials, experiences, and other people they find interesting and compelling in some way. Doing so allows their developing brains to organize information obtained using all of their senses—sight, smell, touch, taste, hearing, vestibular (movement and balance), and proprioception (tells us where body parts are in relation to one another and to other things). A baby's mind and body work in tandem as they experience the environment and everything in it (Berk, 2019). Engaging in this kind of play, they develop new ways of thinking and problem solving, become more efficient at moving about and manipulating objects, and develop better ways of handling their emotions and relating to others (McMullen, 2013; McMullen & Brody, 2021). In this way, play becomes something meaningful not only to the child but also to the care teachers and families that have the privilege of observing it or playing with them.

So meaningful play is achieved when individual babies are allowed to explore freely in a carefully planned environment in which there are play materials that address each baby's individual needs and motivations (Bergen et al., 2008). Babies also need time (more than 15 minutes) to explore the environment, find toys and other objects that interest them, experiment with those things, and practice and consolidate new skills. Of course, the care teacher in the baby room has an important role, but not as trainer of the next developmental milestone or as demonstrator of precisely how to use a toy. Rather, their role is to prepare the environment based upon knowledge of each baby, with suitable materials, furnishings, and equipment; provide support and encouragement for self-exploration; engage in important conversations; and stand ready to scaffold (but not interfere) when necessary.

Invitation for Further Reflection and Discussion

1. In what way is this story related to the well-being senses of engagement and contribution? For instance, what are your thoughts about the well-being of the care teachers who are required to follow this rigid scheduling as it relates to their own experience of engagement and contribution?

2. When I reflected, I said I considered whether what I witnessed in this room was better or worse than simply parking or warehousing the babies during the day. What is your opinion?
3. How did this story make you feel? Have you ever seen something like this? Maybe this example seems extreme to you, but have you ever found yourself being rigid and inflexible about certain things, even in small ways, in how you structure the day in your baby room? Have you been in or seen an environment for very young children that you found overcontrolled?
4. Have you ever worked with someone who was rigid and inflexible? Someone who did not respect the things that you did in the baby room or value your contributions?
5. How would you explain the following ideas that I raised in the reflection: "You can do *too much for* a baby;" "You can do *too much to* a baby;" and "You can do *too little with* a baby."
6. How do you describe "meaningful play"? What is the care teacher's role in this?

CONCLUSION

In the stories in this chapter I presented depictions of adults and children in baby rooms with the purpose of encouraging reflection and discussion of how engagement and contribution impact well-being. I considered the meaning of *engagement* (being able to spend time doing things that are enjoyable, personally meaningful, and intellectually and/or physically stimulating), and of *contribution* (doing things that allow an individual to give of themselves in some way to others). I reflected on several Big Ideas including what empathy and being prosocial looks like for babies, the need to recognize the work and play that occurs in baby rooms as important, and what it means to encourage meaningful play in baby rooms.

CHAPTER 5

Efficacy and Agency

The life stories in this chapter focus on well-being as it relates to experiencing the senses of efficacy and agency in baby rooms. In Chapter 1, Figure 1.1, I showed how my colleagues and I aligned efficacy and agency to the top level of Maslow's (1943) Hierarchy of Needs, referred to as "self-actualization." By placing this at the pinnacle of his pyramid model, Maslow positioned it as the ultimate achievement. *Self-actualization* is described as the realization or fulfillment of one's potential and their coming to understand who they are and act on that knowledge. We interpreted this as an individual feeling capable and confident (efficacy), and free to act on their own behalf (agency).

Remember, however, that in the well-being framework in this book, efficacy and agency are not something to strive for only *after* achieving other elements of well-being. All other elements are equally important (i.e., comfort and security; belonging, respect, and communication; and engagement and contribution). Adults and children in baby rooms need all nine elements of well-being working alongside one another to be and feel an overall sense of well-being physically, psychologically, and emotionally.

UNDERSTANDING THE WELL-BEING SENSES OF EFFICACY AND AGENCY

Efficacy and agency as senses of well-being that I present in this chapter, like the other seven senses, look somewhat different based on the age of the person. The messages received by the individual, however, whether adult or baby, are virtually the same as they are processed by the brain cognitively and emotionally. What is communicated is some version of "I am capable of doing things well" (efficacy) and "I am in control and can take action" (agency).

But like so many of the ways we try to capture complex human feelings and emotions, efficacy and agency are complicated constructs that are difficult to pin down, and dependent, to some extent, upon whom you ask. This is particularly true of agency, which is a term used to think about a variety of other concepts such as diversity, having voice, human capability, autonomy, freedom, and democracy (Cumming & Wong, 2018; Day, 2018; Emirbayer & Mische, 1998; Hart & Brando, 2018; Ratner, 2001; Sorbring, & Kuczynski, 2018; Wright, 2021). While I recognize the complexities of these ideas, in this book I offer a description of the ways I thought about efficacy and agency as I constructed and reflected upon the stories in this chapter.

> *Sense of Efficacy* is experienced when an individual knows there are things they can do well, and they feel generally confident in their abilities, even when trying something new. In addition, they take personal responsibility for their accomplishments, as well as their performance, even when faced with something that challenges or possibly even defeats them. Thus they do not say, "I was just lucky," or "I was only able to do that because it was easy." Rather, they might say, verbally or through gestures, out loud or to themselves, "Look what I did!" or "I did that!" The efficacious individual tends to be motivated by defeat to try again, and in learning something new, will practice doing it to improve performance. Seligman (2011) stressed in his work on flourishing and well-being that all individuals need to feel

capable, and that they are motivated by being able to celebrate their success-es with others. Also, adults and babies need to be presented with tasks at which they *can* succeed that are not completely out of reach. With infants and toddlers, this means providing materials and tasks that constitute a "next step" or challenge, but that will not overly frustrate them into possibly quitting before experiencing success. It also requires that we acknowledge attempts and near misses in things like problem solving during play and when they are learning to interact with peers, thereby encouraging persis-tence and personal pride in accomplishment. My team and I found this to be similar for adults who want to be trusted with important tasks that match as well as recognize their talents and capabilities (McMullen et al., 2020; McCormick et al., 2021). Goouch and Powell (2013) also found that baby room professionals crave receiving recognition for a job well-done. And fi-nally, Lipscomb et al. (2021) warned that a lack of efficacy impacts the well-being of ECCE professionals which in turn effects how they handle work demands and relate to children.

Sense of Agency is experienced when individuals know and feel they can make decisions, are free to make choices about what they do, and take con-trol over those decisions or tasks. Further, according to Paris and Lung (2008), the person with agency has "the ability to see possibilities, as well as a willingness to act, to take initiative . . . [and has] a capacity for self-reflection, self-regulation, and persistence" (p. 255). This is different from, but works in tandem with autonomy, which relates to having the power to act in an intentional manner based upon one's own values, interests, and perceived needs (Paris & Lung, 2008). Although the distinction between agency and autonomy can be confusing, think about autonomy as *having the freedom* to make choices whereas agency is about *acting on that freedom*. For babies, this means that first, we need to let them know they have autonomy—"they have control over themselves and the choices that they make" (Munday, 2018, para. 1)—by setting up environments that foster this (Ridgway et al., 2016). Then we need to relate to them in ways that encour-age them to act on these choices, in other words, to help them be "agents'" of their own actions and outcomes (Basye, 2018). Several early childhood scholars have stressed that encouraging babies and young children to exer-cise their agency is essential in preparing them to live in a democratic society (Gartrell, 2012; Lansdown, 2001). The achievement of a sense of agency is not all that different for care teachers. These adults need to first understand they have autonomy within their environments (or not). If they do, with a sense of agency, they can actively contribute, or be agents in, "shaping their work and its conditions" (Biesta et al., 2015, p. 624).

The life stories in this chapter feature efficacy and agency as they re-late in various ways to confidence that individuals have within themselves of being capable people, including: experiencing a sense of control over one's work and play experiences; having voice in what happens in the baby room and the program; and for care teachers, acquiring knowledge about babies and their families and how children grow, learn, and develop in order to feel confident in their role. As you read the stories, consider the role that the senses of efficacy and agency play in shaping the day-to-day lived experiences of the characters. Also consider if there may be potential for long-term consequences to anyone whose efficacy and agency are not supported.

BABY EMMA, DRUNK WITH POWER

Preamble

This is a composite story featuring the two co-lead care teachers, Jesse and Dylan, introduced in "A Hundred Languages in Baby Rooms" in Chapter 3. It is a composite of events from the Meditation Garden, Wildflower Meadow, and Botanical Garden baby rooms. The story begins with readers meeting Emma, a delightful and fearless 13-month-old girl, and how observing her caused me to watch out for more examples of babies feeling capable, in control, and supported by the care teachers. In addition to Emma, readers will meet Ben and Nancy. I was drawn to Ben and his endless fascination with sorting and ordering things and Nancy's sense of freedom when *not* dressed as a "girly girl." Following the story, I reflect upon the Big Idea of empowering babies through child-centered scaffolding and how that supports the development of a strong and positive sense of self.

Life Story

It was a sunshiny fall day, and I found myself very much enjoying being outside after 2 days stuck inside due to thunderstorms. I love fall days like this in the Midwest, just enough coolness in the air to make the heat of the bright sun welcome, but not too hot; the sky a piercing blue, clear and endless; and the air washed clean by recent rains. The leaves had all just about turned into bright oranges, reds, and yellows, and although most were still on the trees, enough had been blown to the ground by the storms that care teachers were able to rake up small piles for the babies to crinkle, crunch, and jump in. It was while in this space of reverie that I glanced over and saw Emma crawling up the hill to reach the top of the long yellow slide built into a hilly area of the playground.

I had seen Emma crawl/climb to the top of the hill many times. She loved to go down the slide, but only if one of her care teachers held her hand all the way to the bottom. Today, as usual, Emma wanted to do this over and over. As I watched her crawl up the hill for the fourth time since we'd been outside that morning, I thought to myself, "Here we go again." At the top of the hill, she sat with her legs poised to go down the slide. She cried out loudly for someone to help her. A care teacher responded, marched up the hill, and held Emma's hand once again as she scooched her way rather slowly and cautiously to the end of the slide. This time, as Emma reached the bottom, care teacher Jesse said, "This is the last time for a bit, Emma. I need to play with some of our other friends. Why don't you go over and play at the water table with Nancy?" Jesse walked away.

Emma stood still for a full minute or so, watching the back of Jesse as she walked away and settled herself on the ground with two other babies playing in the sand. When Emma turned back toward the hill, the look of determination on her face said to me she was a baby girl on a mission. She crawled to the top and maneuvered so she was sitting at the top of the slide. She looked over at Jesse, who was now sitting on the grass so she could see Emma, but only out of the corner of her eye. Emma stared at Jesse for a minute and then called out—just one screeching yell—and I noticed that Jesse did not turn her head, and did not even make eye contact as she remained busy playing with two other babies. Emma remained still, continuing to stare at Jesse for what must have been only several moments, but for what seemed like forever from where I sat watching.

Eventually, Emma turned her gaze away from Jesse and seemed to trace the trajectory of the slide with her eyes, down its full length and to the ground below. After a few more tense moments, Emma pushed herself off the little seat at the top. Because of the rather slicky quilted one-piece suit she was wearing over her indoor clothes and the fact that no firm hand was holding her back, she slid fast and free all the way to the end, propelled off the ramp, and came to a rather dramatic plop onto the leaf pile at the bottom. I only then realized I had been holding my breath. I watched and waited. Then I heard a sound; "Is she crying?" I thought. No, Emma had started to giggle. She giggled and giggled until it became full, big belly laughs. She then did something quite remarkable, to me at least. She stood up and held her arms out like one of the gymnasts at the Olympics who has just stuck the landing. With her arms out wide, she turned in all directions, making a full circle. When she spotted me and saw I had been watching, she flashed me a wide grin, threw her head back and laughed some more. I laughed too and clapped my hands together silently. Emma then turned toward the hill, and it was up and down the slide over and over, again and again, very confidently, the rest of our time outdoors. I wrote in my notes just after this happened, "Emma, drunk with power." When I spoke to Jesse about what had happened as we were going back inside, she said, "Oh, I noticed, and I was so proud of her. But I knew that this is something Emma needed to do and feel on her own."

"Emma was empowered," I wrote in my field notes. I concluded this was both due to Emma's own desire and courage, found within herself, but also because her care teacher knew just what to do and how much and when to support her. It reminded me of watching as my husband, Rick, decades before, had launched each of our three boys, at different times, into the world of bike riding. He provided a strong hand of support at first and knew just went to let go and let the boys experience the thrill of doing it on their own. Jesse knew that Emma was ready to go down that slide on her own, and not only that, but that she needed to accomplish this herself. By letting go and stepping away, Jesse, like my husband with our boys, gave Emma a precious gift: She allowed Emma the freedom to overcome her fears and to reinforce a self-image that she was capable, brave, and in control. I now had something new to look for in my observations—babies discovering or utilizing the power within themselves to enact plans and accomplish goals, and how this was supported or scaffolded by a knowing care teacher.

Ben was the next baby in the room who caught my attention in this regard. Ben was a quiet and serious little boy of about 17 months. He was not a loner, however, in fact he was a charming and personable little guy. He just mostly seemed to like to play on his own, always so busy and absorbed in his play that he paid little attention to the other children. And he was fascinating to watch. On this particular day, I watched as Ben went from shelf to shelf, basket to basket, all around the room, and brought back toys—stuffed animals, plastic vehicles, colored blocks, small balls, and so on to a spot on the carpet near the window. He made several forays around the room gathering items in a big purse from the dressing area. Each time he returned he dumped the toys in his growing pile of objects. At some point, he seemed satisfied with his little horde of what seemed to me to be unrelated objects. He then got to work. He began putting them in a line that eventually reached about three feet in length.

But it wasn't just a random string of objects he was creating. First came a red truck, then a red ball, followed by a red block. Then a yellow block. Then a yellow school bus and a yellow ducky. The duck preceded several animals of all shapes, colors, and sizes, with each new added item matching at least one attribute of the one before it (i.e., size, shape, color, or category, like animal or vehicle). This seemed to end when Ben added a stuffed plush brown bear toy. Up until now, each time an item was added, Ben stood back and looked thoughtfully at what was at the last item in the row before then deciding what to add next. If he could not find what he needed in his original pile, he surveyed the room carefully before dashing off to collect it. But the brown bear seemed to have him stymied, and it was almost time to clean up before lunch. Care teacher Dylan, who must have been watching this from a distance, quietly walked over to Ben. He held out a small, molded plastic polar bear and said, "Would this help? Could it be the end of your train?" Ben smiled at Dylan, took the toy, and added it to the others. He then brushed his hands together in an "all done" sort of gesture, seemingly satisfied that he was done with his work. I asked Dylan later how he knew this would help him. "I learned a long time ago in working with Ben," he said, "to mostly stand back and let him do what he's going to do. It's always something amazing. But I also know that if he can't figure something out, it doesn't take too long for him to become frustrated and feel defeated."

Also, in this room was a 12-month-old baby girl named Nancy. My first impression of her was that she was a hesitant, shy child, maybe temperamentally what some might label, *slow-to-warm-up*. (This was to become yet another lesson in my life of not being too hasty to label a child.) On the day I first met Nancy, she arrived dressed as if for a party. I soon learned that this is how she always started her day. She typically arrived wearing beautiful, frilly, and expensive-looking dresses, shiny patent leather shoes, and white or pink tights. Her father brought her in each day and waited until everyone "oohed" and "ahhhed," and told Nancy how very beautiful she looked in whatever she had on. It was clear that this made the care teachers uncomfortable, but they did it nonetheless to satisfy Dad.

On the first day I met her, I noticed that after Nancy went in for her first diaper change, she came out wearing more typical play clothes, and furthermore, she seemed to carry herself with a decidedly new attitude. Gone was the baby I thought to be shy and hesitant, replaced by an active baby who seemed ready to take on the world. As I was to find out, at the end of the day, 15 minutes before Dad would come to pick her up, "exuberant Nancy" was changed back into "fancy Nancy." Care teacher Dylan filled me in: "We tried talking to both Mom and Dad about this. Mom understands, but she leaves before Dad gets Nancy ready in the morning and feels reluctant to disagree with how dad dresses her. So, this is what we worked out with Mom."

What Dylan and Jesse told me they were most concerned about was that the dressy clothes Nancy arrived in restricted her movement and made things like managing the stairs and ramp on the climber dangerous. Further, Jesse told me, "In the early days when we had left her in the dress, we [the adults] began to realize we never put out messy things, like paint of any kind, glue, markers, and shaving cream, and we were constantly worried she would ruin her clothes outside, so we steered her to do only quiet and clean things." But now, from what I observed, Nancy loved to do anything messy—the messier the better—and usually needed quite a washing before being put back in her dress, tights, and Mary Janes, and assuming her more demure attitude.

Reflection—Empowering Babies Through Child-Centered Scaffolding

As I finished writing this story and reflected upon it, the Big Idea that jumped out at me was that the teachers empowered the babies by scaffolding their play and that the scaffolding was unique to the needs of the individual babies. The babies were allowed, first and foremost, to play freely and make choices about what they needed and wanted to do. This supported their autonomy, which according to Jung and Recchia (2013) and Munday (2018) has to do with having the power to act intentionally based upon one's own interests and needs. *Doing* the actions is the exercising of agency. Trevarthen and Delafield-Butt (2017) described this as, "seeking understanding of what to do with body and mind in a world of invented possibilities" (p. 17). The care teachers allowed the babies autonomy in terms of uninterrupted periods of free play, which gave Emma, Ben, and Nancy opportunities to exercise their agency. Doing so, they became more efficacious about their abilities to perform various tasks and skills—physically, cognitively, and emotionally.

Important in this story is that each of the babies had care teachers, in this case Jesse and Dylan, who recognized them as unique individuals with their own particular needs and motivations. Further, they recognized that sometimes this required them, as observant adults, to step in (Ben), at other times to step away (Emma), and in some cases to remove constraints (Nancy). Each is scaffolding, as I see it, supporting the description given by Gillespie and Greenberg (2017) who said: "Scaffolding is how adults support children's development and learning by offering just the right help at just the right time in just the right way" (p. 90).

Similarly, Jung and Recchia (2013) found that the care teachers of infants they studied thought deeply about how best to support infant play and considered when and how to scaffold babies according to their individual needs and learning styles. The ways they spoke of scaffolding to empower babies resonated with how I felt about the care teachers in this story. Emma, Ben, and Nancy were scaffolded differently, and as a result, empowered in ways that recognized their unique needs. It demonstrated to me that the care teachers had thought deeply about each individual child. Williams and her colleagues (2010) referred to this as "child-centered scaffolding" (p. 251). Care teachers must remain alert and watchful, paying close attention to those moments in which their involvement or intervention will be helpful. But they must be careful not to interrupt or interfere with the child's experience of succeeding on their own. As Singer and her colleagues (2014) found, to be most beneficial to the child, care teachers must remain nearby and alert, and must carefully consider the right moment to insert themselves—if at all.

The idea of "child-centered scaffolding" made me revisit my understanding of Vygotskian notions of scaffolding and the Zone of Proximal Development (ZPD) (Vygotsky, 1978). According to Vygotsky scholars Bodrova and Leong (2007) ZPD "is a distance between the actual developmental level determined by individual problem solving and the level of development as determined through problem solving under guidance or in collaboration with more capable peers" (p. 212). Put more simply, it is the distance between what the baby or child can do on their own and what they may be able to do if they have help from a friend or an adult or some material. That "help" is the scaffolding. My lived experiences in baby rooms has led me to interpret definitions of *scaffolding* and *ZPD* more broadly than in the past. I now see the role of the adult in "helping" as more varied and dependent upon their knowledge of each child. Reflecting upon my experiences has helped me (scaffolded me!) to conclude that a child's positive sense of self is not so much about helping them get to the top of their ZPD *as we define it*. Rather, it is about following their lead and supporting them to have success, *as they see it*, in their own self-guided endeavors. For this, children need to have knowledgeable, mindful, and sensitively responsive adults around them in baby rooms.

Invitation for Further Reflection and Discussion

1. In the chapter introduction I used a shorthand way to describe the senses of well-being featured: "I am capable of doing things well" (efficacy) and "I am in control and can take action" (agency). Describe how Emma, Ben, and Nancy experienced a sense of efficacy, and consider how that is different from their experience of a sense of agency.
2. Can you think of an example of how you have supported efficacy and agency in a child?
3. How do you feel about what the care teachers and Nancy's mother did by working together to go around Nancy's father? In essence, they were participating together in a deception. Are there ever circumstances when that is okay? Would you have done something different?
4. You might say that in their own way, each of the three babies featured—Emma, Ben, and Nancy—experienced being "drunk with power." What do you think I mean by that? Have you ever witnessed this? Have you ever felt that way yourself?
5. Is empowerment of a baby or a young child always a good thing? In other words, can they become *too* empowered? If so, what would that look like to you?

6. In Chapter 2's story "When Not Just Anyone Will Do" and in the reflection for Chapter 4's "Training Starfish Babies to 'Play,'" I speak of "doing too much for" and "doing too little with" a baby. It is sometimes hard for care teachers to balance these two, and to "do what is just right for" a child. Did the care teachers in this story achieve the right balance? Is this a challenge for you? How would you advise another care teacher struggling with this?

EMPOWERED DECISION-MAKERS

Preamble

This story brings up issues of who holds the power to make decisions about what happens in baby rooms and how that power impacts or is impacted by the care teachers, children, and families sharing the space. I revisit the Meditation Garden Program with co-lead care teachers, Lily Grace and Lisa, featured in Chapter 2's "A Place for Baby and Mom." I highlight the shared-power structure in which multiple voices are involved in decision-making. In the reflection, I consider the Big Idea of shared power, specifically, how this shows respect for the agency of the individuals and the resulting impact on their experience of efficacy.

Life Story

When I arrived for my 1st day to conduct research at the Meditation Garden Program, I was met at the door by Rosaria, the administrator. Rosaria gave me a warm smile and welcomed me enthusiastically. She ushered me in through the password-secured entrance and I signed in. We walked down the hall past a small kitchen and two multiage preschool rooms. We stopped briefly so I could see the cozy-looking lactation room before she led me into the infant/toddler wing of the building. Along the way we encountered staff, families, and children of various ages engaged in the normal hustle and bustle of starting the day. There were many warm and friendly greetings exchanged between Rosaria and others. I was impressed by how well Rosaria knew everyone and addressed all adults and children by name. I took notice of how, rather than being known as "Mrs. Keller," she was on a first-name basis with children and adults alike. As we approached the baby room, the door flew open and out popped a little boy who I later learned had transitioned to elementary school a few weeks before. He and his mother had just dropped off his baby sister. When he saw us, he shouted, "Rosaria!" and threw himself into her arms where he received a big hug in return and lots of questions about how he liked 1st grade.

Before entering the baby room, Rosaria and I slipped off our outdoor shoes. She put on slippers that were her own, stored in a little shelf with her name on it by the door. I took off my shoes and decided to go in socked feet rather than wear the shoe covers provided. As we walked in, we were greeted warmly by Lily Grace who was introduced as one of the two co-lead care teachers of the baby room. "Interesting," I thought. "Co-leads? What's that all about?" The notion of co-leads was relatively new to me. Most programs I knew had care teams that consisted of a lead and assistant who worked together with one or more full- or part-time aides. In my experience the lead care teacher was expected to be more highly qualified in terms of education and experience, and with the title came a larger salary and greater responsibilities.

When I joined Lily Grace in the staff lounge during her lunch break and planning time, she provided initial thoughts on why she liked the co-lead structure. For one, she said, "We share all the tasks." She also liked the co-lead structure because, as she explained: "Now, we are able to schedule it so that mom or dad can talk to a lead [care] teacher when they come in the morning *and* at the end of the day. They get to know both of us very well." In a follow-up conversation, I asked Lily Grace to explain how a major decision like this, the adoption of the co-lead model, was made and by whom. I asked: "Were you all just told one day that from now on this is what we're doing?"

Through several conversations with Lily Grace, her co-lead care teacher, Lisa, and the program administrator, Rosaria, I learned much about the organizational structure surrounding and including those in the baby room and about how decisions—big and small—tended to be made. First, in terms of everyday practice, as Lily Grace described it, there were never any "orders from above" about what to do and how to do it. She said they were "trusted" as professionals to know "best practices" and to "engage appropriately" with babies and families, and that as professionals working in the Meditation Garden Program, they "faithfully followed the child-centered, play-based philosophy of the program." Rosaria, hearing this, smiled at Lily Grace and added, "We hire only the best people and trust them to know what they're doing." Turning to me she said, with some seriousness, "I'm here to help and support them, not micromanage their every move."

So, no "big" decisions and changes were simply handed down "from above," as Lily Grace had phrased it. Rather, she said, it was "everyone's responsibility to participate" in deciding upon, planning, and implementing changes such as the move to the co-lead structure, or years earlier when transitioning to a full continuity of care model across ages birth to

3 years. I spent a long time thinking about what she said and how she said it, impressed by how she saw it as a "responsibility" to participate in decision-making. I wrote in my notes: "Like the responsibilities we have as democratic citizens." Care teachers, and others, such as families, did not feel that they had to raise their voices and shout to be heard, but rather, as members of this community, it was their responsibility to remain engaged.

It became clear to me that big decisions were not made rashly, nor was the leadership performed in a top-down manner. Rather, this and other major decisions that impacted the baby room, and other rooms in the program, seemed to involve a continuous swirling of ideas back and forth, up-and-down, side-to-side as they were deliberated on over time by all constituents. Probing further, I learned about various entities in which ideas and proposals for changes were considered—through informal conversations among care teachers in the staff lounge; during weekly staff meetings; at the monthly advisory council meetings for the Meditation Garden Program; and in a university ECCE coalition meeting held 3 to 4 times a year. At all levels of consideration of ideas and major decisions, members of the baby room (staff and families) were either present themselves or represented by Rosaria. For example, a family member and one of the co-lead care teachers from the baby room (and all other rooms) served on the advisory council, and Rosaria and all other administrators from each of the campus childcare programs were members of the university ECCE coalition. This system encouraged discussion, careful consideration, and buy-in from all who would be impacted.

I learned that the change to the co-lead model was one of those decisions that swirled up and down and sideways through the system for quite some time, years in fact. All this time was spent identifying other programs who had implemented this model and "picking their brains," deliberating on the potential impact—positive or negative—for all involved and holding multiple discussions with financial officers and other administrators about how to pay for it. In the end, it was decided that it was important to do to achieve greater equity among qualified professionals. It was also done to respect the fact that both lead and assistant childcare staff throughout the system at that time were expected to have bachelor's degrees and experience when hired. A major driver of the decision was that although both leads and assistants had essentially the same job expectations and duties, the lead was paid substantially more than the assistant. A new wage structure was created that recognized seniority in educational attainment and years of experience but that equalized base pay upon hiring. The practical day-to-day implications of having co-leads was that no one person was the boss or the in-the-room supervisor of the other, but rather they were to be equal partners.

This all sounded marvelous to me—shared decision-making at all levels; everyone's voices heard and included at the table; and partners sharing the burden of decision-making in the baby room and being recognized as equals by title and compensation. But I wondered how coleads in the room works in terms of who does what and who really makes the decisions. I was especially curious about how notions of "control" and "equality" were lived out in this room where I knew that one of the care teachers had more education and experience than the other. I jotted these questions in my research journal and set out to see if I could answer them by the end of my time there.

Lily Grace's colead care teacher, Lisa, was a relatively young ECCE professional with a bachelor's degree and 3 years of experience. When I asked, Lisa told me she "loved" the colead structure. "But" she went on, "even though Lily Grace is not my 'boss,' she is absolutely my mentor. I have learned so much from her." (Lily Grace had over 25 years of experience and had a master's degree in ECCE.) In our conversations, Lisa explained that as she saw it, she and Lily Grace were equal partners in terms of making decisions about routines, room arrangements, adjustments to schedules and other practicalities, as well as the basic style they had of responding sensitively and respectfully to each baby as an individual. They divided up responsibilities for record-keeping, were "key persons" for an equal number of babies/families, and worked together on planning and assessments, as well as in conducting formal care teacher/family conferences.

As I observed Lily Grace and Lisa in action, they really did appear to work together well, in fact nearly seamlessly as a team, often anticipating each other's actions, responses, and needs. When I told Lisa what I observed, she said, "Yes, we're excellent partners." She went on, "Lily Grace has so much wisdom and experience. I look to her to give me advice about things I'm less comfortable with, like sometimes how to talk to parents when I have a concern. She helps me work through it and helps me decide how best to do it." Clearly, "equal" partnerships are complex things. Lily Grace, for her part, although highly positive about her colead arrangement with Lisa, was realistic about the challenges. "It takes time," she said, "for good partnerships to gel so they work well together. It takes work. It doesn't just happen." There was a pause as she seemed to think about it for a few moments before adding, "But, it is well worth the effort."

I end this story where I began, with Rosaria, the program administrator. I came to see her as the linchpin, empowering everyone to feel their voices were heard and respected. She established a climate where all members of their childcare community, children and adults, were empowered with a sense of control over what happened, had the freedom to exercise choice, and were encouraged to express their needs and opinions. Rosaria was expert in amplifying the voices of the staff, families, and children of the Meditation Garden Program throughout the campus and into the surrounding community. As administrator, she of course sometimes had to make tough choices and communicate disappointing news when realities of things like health and safety codes, licensing regulations, accreditation standards, or campus officials got in the way of some of the community's dreams. But, like all else, she did this with grace and compassion. My last words about this in my journal were, "Every program needs a Rosaria."

Reflection—Shared Power in Decision-Making

This story from the Meditation Garden Program, speaks to me about the Big Idea of shared power in decision-making and how this shows respect for all individuals involved. The opportunity I had to observe such a system up close, and how it seemed to make all involved thrive and flourish, led me to consider connections between individuals' well-being and the leadership style of an organization. In this system, autonomous practice in day-to-day, moment-to-moment decision-making by baby room care teachers was the norm, as was full participation in deliberation on bigger, broader issues of impact to the whole program. Care teachers were not just welcomed to the table but expected to show up and engage fully. As Lily Grace had said, "it was their responsibility to participate." In a very real sense, the system supported care teachers, and others including families, to be agents who, if not in full control, had at least some input over what happened in the program. I believe that this contributed to what I found to be true in the care teachers— they were "efficacious" in terms of being highly confident in their practices with babies and families and in interactions and work projects with professional colleagues.

When reflecting on this, I reread some of the work from Anne Douglass, a highly regarded scholar who studies ECCE leadership. Douglass considers what she refers to as "organizational systems" which are the contexts in which decisions are made and power is distributed in childcare programs. Of interest to me, given my experience in this baby room and others like it since, are Douglass's ideas contrasting "relational" and "conventional" bureaucracies within ECCE organizational systems. In Douglass's 2011 article, she compares them in this way:

> *Relational Bureaucracy*: Democratic and participatory structures provide opportunities to share knowledge, expertise, and power. Systems exist to support use of relational competencies for caring, flexible, and responsive approaches to individual needs. Relational competencies are recognized, valued, and developed.

Conventional Bureaucracy: Hierarchical staff structures recognize a hierarchy of expertise, knowledge, and power. Rigid rules, boundaries, and policies exist to guide a uniform approach. Staff relationships are formal, hierarchical, and impersonal. Adherence to rules and protocol is recognized and valued.

In the Meditation Garden, I had the opportunity to see in action a relational bureaucracy, or what Douglass in later writings (2018) referred to as a "relational organizational culture and climate." It was certainly democratic and participatory, and it valued competencies related to building and maintaining relationships.

I realize that based upon the stories I have shared in the previous chapters of this book, some readers may be wondering how the relational model portrayed here compares to what I experienced in the Laboratory Greenhouse Program. As you might guess, the descriptors for the conventional bureaucracy very closely fit that program. I chose this time, however, to focus on what I considered the highly positive example of organizational context and leadership I found in the Meditation Garden Program. I did this very specifically because I wanted to show how a relationship-based power structure *can* and *does* exist in real life. Many of us have probably experienced systems that fall short of the example of a relational bureaucracy, but I hope that at least a few of you have experienced one that was a sharp contrast to the Laboratory Greenhouse Program.

Granted, just by what I have said, I am making a value judgment about what I position as "good" and "bad" or "positive" and "negative" in terms of running an ECCE program. That is true; I admit the bias, and I own it. To me this is an issue of recognizing the human dignity and personhood of all individuals within a system, and it aligns with the well-being lens through which I view such things. I find support for this from Douglass (2016) who describes relational systems as "including compassion, mutual support, and participants' ability to make sense of, adapt to, and positively contribute" (p. 211). Douglass went on to claim that such processes are not only good for the individuals involved, but that they "strengthen collective resilience in the early care and education field" (p. 211). To me, this is something worth fighting for.

Invitation for Further Reflection and Discussion

1. How did Rosaria and the system empower individuals as problem-solvers and decision-makers? What does that have to do with efficacy and agency?
2. Imagine the situation in which all the power comes from the top (the administrator or someone above or outside the program)

and decisions are handed down to you, a professional in a baby room. You have little or no choice in what you can do and how you do it on a day-to-day basis, and you are unable or unwelcome to participate in programwide planning and problem solving. How would this impact your senses of efficacy and agency?

3. What are the decision-making processes you have experienced in ECCE? Were they more relational or conventional in terms of its structures and processes? Do you feel the one described in this story would work where you are now? If not, why?

4. What clues did you get from the beginning of the story about the leadership style of this program based on what I shared about my time with Rosaria when I arrived on the first day? What did it tell you about the "leadership climate" in this program? How is this like or different from your own program or ones you have visited?

5. Are you familiar with the idea of "co-lead" care teachers? If so, what has been your experience with this structure? If this is new to you, what do you think of the idea? Explain.

6. Are you familiar with other forms of shared responsibility between care teachers? For instance, some programs may rotate leadership responsibilities. Or some may be structured so that one is a lead on some things, and another a lead for others. What are your thoughts on this? Can you think of some other ways to share baby room leadership that are fair to each individual?

7. I came to believe that the relational bureaucracy I experienced was reminiscent of values we try to uphold in American-style democracy. Do you see this? Explain.

KNOWLEDGE IS POWER

Preamble

In this story, I have returned to the Wildflower Meadow Baby Room after my initial research (see Chapter 4) to spend time in discussion with care teachers and family members about continuity of care. It is a story about the power of knowledge formed through relationships with one another in this program and how that contributes to a sense of efficacy in its participants. I use the actual words of the characters as they share their thoughts about their lived experiences with continuity of care. Some of the quotations used have been previously published (McMullen et al., 2015). Following the story, I reflect upon the Big Idea of power that comes from long-term relationships.

Life Story

When I came back to the Wildflower Meadow Baby Room to study continuity of care as practiced in this program, I had already established a relationship with this community during my earlier research. I had an easy rapport with the baby room co-lead care teachers and a great deal of respect for them as professionals, having seen them in action with children and families. At the time of this visit, both were working on their master's degrees, and each had well over a decade of experience. Further, they were in their third 3-year cycle of continuity with a group of children and families. I knew there was so much they could teach me!

Wildflower Meadow used a continuity of care model known as "looping." Babies and the care team stayed together from the time they entered the program, usually when the babies were only a few weeks to a few months old, until the summer after their 3rd birthday. As 3-year-olds, they transitioned into the multiage preschool program for 3- to 5-year-olds. So, babies, families, and care teachers really got to know each other well over the 3 years or so they spent together. As Monica, one of the parents said to me, "We're all in this together!" Monica further described what she appreciated most about continuity, contrasting it with the more "traditional" practice, which she referred to as the "revolving door." (In the traditional model, babies are grouped by age and transition to a new room based upon reaching a developmental milestone like walking, being toilet-trained, or having a birthday. Therefore, babies are frequently transitioning in and out of the room.) Monica had experienced a traditional program with her first baby:

> Well, in the traditional revolving-door model you have to start over again and again, so it's kind of like getting a new family doctor, you know? You've got to tell him the whole history. This is what he [first baby] likes, this is what he does, this is what you should know about what he doesn't like, don't make him do this. . . . Like you know, I feel like it is kind of starting over. Whereas this year . . . there was no me getting to know them, no her [second baby] getting to know them. So, to not have to go through that every year is brilliant! (McMullen et al., 2015, p. 15)

Monica's metaphor of going to the doctor's office struck a chord with me. Like many of you reading this, I have experienced the frustration of starting over again with new physicians who don't know me. This spoke to me of how knowing someone well as an individual is important.

When I asked Vivian about her perspective on continuity practices as a care teacher, she said:

The best thing . . . is watching the process. It's watching the developmental process from really the beginning, and being able to see it through until children reach a completely different level and being able to document that and talk it over with families, and I mean, there's so much discovery and growth that happens 0 to 3. It's *amazing* to get to be an observer and participant in that. (McMullen et al., 2015, p. 14)

I really appreciated Vivian's phrasing of being a "participant in" what happens over the first three years. Mentioning this to Vivian and Lucy over lunch one day, they looked at each other, and one kind of shrugged. I interpreted their initial silence and body language as saying, "Does she not get it?" Lucy then turned to me and said, "We don't view babies as lesser beings, but as full, capable human beings, deserving of our respect. We participate *with* them in the process." I quickly clarified that I absolutely agreed with this sentiment and was just sharing how much I admired the way they spoke of babies as contributing members of their community. They went on to chat with me about issues of respect for the personhood of all people, big and small, and echoed Monica's comment that, "We're all in this together."

Following up on the idea of everyone being "in this together," I asked Vivian and Lucy about "working with" families. Lucy explained that being "in this together," meant just that—that the care teachers participated *with* babies and *with* families and that they participate *with* them. Vivian expanded on this, quite passionately, with her view that a key to working with families was to encourage them to talk openly to them about their hopes, concerns, beliefs, and goals for their children:

We want our parents empowered! We're always advocating for parents to . . . speak their minds about their children's educational experiences, about their children's social experience, about everything that goes on for their child. We tell them from the beginning that they're their child's first advocate. This is your child. Speak up for your child! Speak up for what you feel is right! If you see that something is going on in your heart, you know that it should be different, don't be shy. (McMullen et al., 2015, p. 14)

This expectation to engage fully seemed to be understood by the families. As Meredith, a mother of a baby girl said to me later,

I feel very comfortable talking to them [care teachers] about any concern I might have or expressing things that I like that they're doing, or I want to make sure that, you know, I'm doing my part and whatever. And they have expectations of the parents. (McMullen et al., 2015, p. 14)

Another mother, Debra, likened what the care teachers did to "an investment," in the relationship they had with families, and spoke of them as "allies" in parenting:

> I felt that the [care] teachers had an investment, like they really cared about my child, and they were invested in providing this long-term kind of support for him . . . it was just, they knew those kids so well. So, I think for me the benefit of continuity of care was just the high level of investment in the relationship. I considered the teachers more than our allies, kind of like our, you know, another set of parents. (McMullen data from field journal, 2013)

The nature of the relationships that the care teachers formed with the babies was something that family members remarked upon frequently. They described how the relationships instilled in them a sense of confidence that their children were "in good hands." Dao-Ming, mother of a baby boy, described it this way: "They have really warm, loving relationships with all the kids . . . it makes me very confident and comfortable. I'm really, really happy for him to have [care teachers] who he feels very securely attached to." One of the fathers, Demetri, told me that he and his wife had great confidence in the care teachers because of their attentiveness, knowledge, and skill:

> We were just so, so impressed by the attention and the interest and the skill of both Vivian and Lucy. I mean, I've never seen anything like it. You know, the way that they would just day after day give us detailed reports about what was going on with her, they really knew so many things about her. (McMullen et al., 2015, p. 14)

After speaking to these parents, I sat in the staff lounge to gather my thoughts about all that I was learning. Jack, a care teacher nearing the end of a 3-year continuity cycle in another room sat down, and we began to chat. I shared with him what I was learning and asked him what he found to be the biggest benefit to continuity. He told me, "Long-term relationships" and "really getting to know the children well" was the most important aspect of continuity of care. He further explained:

> I know these children so well since starting with them. When you get to know these children this well you can see where they're going. Just being able to know, literally just know, *that* child over there, right now, I could put them to bed now, they've had a pacifier since they came . . . and know within a week that child is ready [to give up the pacifier] . . . and be 100% accurate. We're starting potty training, and again, it's like, *this* child's ready, *that* child's not. (McMullen et al., 2015, p. 14)

But it wasn't just adults whose confidence was supported through these long-term relationships; nearly everyone I spoke to stressed it was the children who benefited most of all. Jack, for instance, said, "Continuity of care really builds an emotional platform, stability, a foundation that those children can use." I asked a preschool teacher, Tatsu, who works with the children after they turn 3 and transition into her room, "How do the children from the continuity program compare to others when they start in your room?" She told me: "The children who were in the [continuity program] together, socially, emotionally, and in terms of the development of self-help skills, are more confident in those areas." She described it as the children that came from continuity infant/toddler program were able to "hit the ground running" in terms of how they play, use the resources in the room, and interact with other children and the adults. And, she added, the same is true of the families. "They do not hesitate to talk to us about their concerns. They are *very* empowered."

I came away from the experience feeling quite confident about promoting continuity of care as a model for care and education in birth-to-3. "It really works!" I wrote in my journal. But I added a cautionary note to myself about how what I experienced was continuity in a program recognized for its quality by the state and through national accreditation. It was a "mature" program with highly qualified professionals. I concluded that continuity of care is something not to be entered into quickly; it requires careful deliberation over time with everyone involved—professional staff and families.

Reflection—The Power of Long-Term Relationships

Sir Francis Bacon (1561–1626), considered the father of the scientific method is credited as the first to say, in his 1579 book *Meditationes Sacrae* (Rodrígez García, 2001), "Knowledge is power." As an educator and ongoing learner, I think of that phrase often. Knowledge *is* power. Three simple words—but to me they are, well, powerful! I thought of them often as I reflected on this story. The care teachers felt confident and powerful from knowledge gained about the children and the families over time. The parents felt comfortable and confident in the care teachers because of the knowledge and skills they demonstrated. The babies were building a firm foundation upon social, emotional, cognitive, and self-help knowledge and skills developed and practiced, which made them more powerful and better prepared to take on the challenges of transitioning to preschool. And all of this was possible, or at least enhanced, by spending 3 years together as a group of care teachers, babies, and families during those first three very important years of the children's lives.

The power came from the intimate knowledge of one another gained through long-term relationships, the Big Idea of this reflection. This resulted in efficacy, as I characterized it earlier, demonstrated in the confident way they expressed themselves. The care teachers' words in the story, and those of many I interviewed, revealed highly confident professionals. Family members I talked to spoke of their confidence as advocates and partners with the care teachers in the care and education of their children. Because of this, the babies who were cared for and educated lovingly and confidently by the care teachers and families were themselves active, confident, risk-taking, and persistent in their endeavors. In short, all involved seemed highly efficacious.

The many benefits of continuity of care in birth-to-3 settings have been documented for the last 2 decades in the research (Ackerman, 2008; Cryer et al., 2000; Garrity et al., 2015; Horm et al., 2018; McMullen et al., 2016), but its widespread adoption in practice in the United States is yet to be seen. I documented many of its benefits in McMullen (2018), as have others, including that continuity of care

- Deepens care teacher knowledge of individual children and as a result, sensitivity of responsiveness to them (Recchia, 2012; Ruprecht et al., 2015)
- Increases care teacher knowledge of child development (Ackerman, 2008; Horm et al., 2018)
- Increases knowledge and understanding of families including how their children are cared for in the context of their home life, community, and culture (Raikes & Edwards, 2009; Reidt-Parker & Chainski, n.d.)
- Facilitates secure attachments in children (Raikes, 1996)
- Supports early peer relationships (Elicker et al., 2014; McMullen et al., 2009)
- Supports smoother, more even developmental progress with fewer regressions and behavioral issues (Ruprecht et al., 2015)
- Decreases child, family, and care teacher stress that results from multiple transitions (Cryer et al., 2005; Zero to Three, 2010)
- Strengthens care teacher–family partnerships and empowers families (Anderson, 2018; McMullen & Apple, 2012)

When I have promoted continuity of care to some ECCE professionals at workshops and conferences, I have experienced push back from individuals who cite many potential hurdles to implementing it in their programs (Aguillard et al., 2005; Hegde & Cassidy, 2004). Although all concerns are legitimate and to be taken seriously, most of what I have heard seems to fall into the categories of the "fear of change" and thus "fear of the unknown." In McMullen (2017), I present several of the concerns and challenges I have heard, including:

- *"Families won't like it."* In my experience, they love it.
- *"Care teachers won't like it."* Again, I have found the opposite to be true once it is implemented and running well.
- *"What if I get stuck with a care teacher I don't like"* (family) or *"What if I get stuck with a family I don't like"* (care teachers). Several care teachers and family members have told me that this was a fear they had when they first implemented continuity of care but that those fears were quickly put aside. They explained to me that when care teachers and families realize they will be working together (or "stuck" together) for a long time, they become more invested in working on their relationships.
- *"Life is change; they [the babies] better get used to it."* This one is so silly to me, that I remember the first time it came up I was speechless. Just because something is going to happen in middle school or high school does not mean it is appropriate for babies. A wise colleague of mine, childcare teacher, administrator, and advocate Tim Dunnuck, once said to me, "Mary, you don't prepare them for a hurricane by putting them through a hurricane!" Of course, he's right; you prepare for a hurricane by putting down sandbags, gathering your resources like food and bottled water, making a plan to evacuate if necessary, and so on. In much the same way, we need to prepare the babies in our care by arming them with the emotional tools, problem-solving skills, self-confidence, and other resources to navigate through their own future storms.
- Finally, *"It's too difficult."* It is hard work, but it is not too difficult if you are "all in it together." It takes a community of dedicated professionals and families to come together to do the work, a community committed to doing what is best for children.

Although moving to full continuity is not simple, and like so many things in life that are worth doing, it takes effort. It takes study, deliberation, and planning before implementation. It takes maintenance and constant scrutiny as it proceeds. Some birth-to-3 programs, upon self-evaluation, may find they are not ready, or they may determine there are other, higher priorities that need attention first. As I have written, continuity of care "is the icing on the cake for an already strong, quality setting, serving to increase the overall quality and ensure the best possible experiences for children as they live, love, work, and play through their days in infant/toddler childcare settings" (McMullen, 2017, p. 49). Although it may take time to implement continuity, each step forward improves the lived experience of childcare for the babies, families, and care teachers. It is well worth the effort!

Invitation for Further Reflection and Discussion

1. Agency is not mentioned explicitly in this story or reflection. What is the role of agency in this scenario? Could the efficacy expressed as "confidence" in the care teachers, families, and babies have existed without their experiencing a sense of agency?
2. Increased care teacher knowledge of child development is listed as a benefit of continuity of care in birth to age 3. How might that occur?
3. Do you have experience with continuity of care in your current program? Or did you in a prior position or perhaps in a program you have visited? Was it a looping or multiage model? Describe what you experienced. Was your experience positive or negative? Explain.
4. Think about what the mother Monica said about the "revolving door" of childcare being like constantly having to build a new relationship with a doctor. Have you experienced this? How did it feel? On the flip side, if you have had the doctor for many years, what have been the advantages?
5. If you are not in a continuity setting, are you ready to try it? Why or why not? If your program does engage in continuity practices, describe how it started and how it is going. What are the concerns and challenges you or your program may need to (or have) overcome to do this?

CONCLUSION

Through the life stories in this chapter, I explored the lived experiences of care teachers, administrators, families, and babies as I considered the well-being elements of efficacy and agency. I encouraged you to reflect upon and discuss your own experiences with these constructs and to think about the role of efficacy and agency in your own well-being. I started the chapter by presenting a shorthand way to understand the terms efficacy ("I am capable of doing things well") and agency ("I am in control and can take action"). Then with the life stories I illustrated several Big Ideas including the following: empowering babies through child-centered scaffolding, shared power in decision-making, and the power of long-term relationships.

CHAPTER 6

Closing Thoughts

The stories in this book have been with me for a long time, some for over a decade. Reading through old notes, poring through photographs and videos as I prepared to write allowed me not only to reminisce, but to relive and experience afresh the strong emotional connection I had with the various characters and events at the time. Some of those emotions were highly positive—like the feeling you get when catching up with dear old friends; whereas some of the stories caused me to revisit feelings that were not so pleasant. But in taking this journey to share my stories and some of my thoughts about them, I experienced an overall sense of satisfaction, cognitively as well as emotionally.

I also admit to feeling proud of myself for taking what, for me, felt like a risk. Telling these stories and sharing my thoughts and emotions makes me feel somehow vulnerable and exposed. I am willing to bet some of you reading this have felt this way from time to time about sharing your thoughts and feelings. But I also know that any of you who have spent time with babies and young children have your own stories, and for some of you, they are bursting to be told. Whether your stories are funny or poignant, or speak of challenges or triumphs, they all have the power to be insightful, informative, and sometimes transformative. I urge you to find a way to tell your stories, if not for a book, article, or blog, share them with your colleagues and those you mentor. This advice is a distant echo of words spoken by Vivian Gussin Paley (1929–2019), one of my personal ECCE sheroes, in an interview with the *American Journal of Play* (2009):

> We must become anecdotists and storytellers. Where do educators begin our practice of becoming anecdotists and storytellers? The opportunities are many: in our schools of education, in our faculty rooms, at our parent-teacher conferences, and above all, in the classroom with our children and fellow teachers. (p. 128)

If sharing your stories feels threatening or uncomfortable for any reason, at least consider writing them out for yourself. I have always loved the following quotation attributed to writer Joan Didion because it speaks to the highly personal aspects of the writing process and its value in helping us make meaning of our sometimes jumbled thoughts and feelings: *"I write entirely to find out what I'm thinking, what I'm looking at, what I see and what it means"* (quoted by Sutton, 2011, p. 20).

With this sentiment in mind—writing to "find out what I'm thinking"—I want to share my thoughts on why I chose to include so many negative stories in this book. Specifically, featuring so many stories from the Laboratory Greenhouse Baby Room was a tough decision because I realize that the experiences that I related may seem extreme (I hope) to most readers. As I said at the beginning of Chapter 2, it is sometimes helpful when trying to understand something to consider its opposite. For me personally, it was important to share these stories because in writing them down, I was reminded about how much I learned from these negative experiences. In her 1994 book, *Power and Emotion in Infant-Toddler Day Care*, Robin Leavitt also included examples of negative or "bad" interactions with babies along with positive ones. Doing so provided readers a more comprehensive exploration of themes central to her book including emotional responsiveness, empowered care, and the need for care teacher self-reflection.

Part of why I found it troubling to include so many negative examples of practices in baby rooms was that, as I said in Chapter 1, I wanted to maintain a posture of "goodness" in this writing (Lawrence-Lightfoot, 2005; Lawrence-Lightfoot & Davis, 1997). If you recall, I said that even if my tone was critical, I would try not to be overly judgmental. In the end, this was very hard and, as a result, I am sure it is clear to the reader how conflicted I felt about certain experiences. But a goodness perspective is not one in which everything must be portrayed in a rosy and positive light. Rather, it suggests to me that I needed to give the characters in the stories the benefit of the doubt and believe their intentions were "good." I am confident that no one I observed had any intention to do harm to any baby, even though I disagreed, sometimes strongly, with some of the practices they implemented.

I asked you to be charitable in considering the actions and behaviors of characters I portrayed. What are the circumstances and constraints under which various characters featured in the stories in the Laboratory Greenhouse Baby Room may be working (i.e., in terms of environment and infrastructure, level of knowledge and expertise, policies, administrative support, and so on)? Remember these stories included "Through the Looking Glass" (Chapter 2), "Teddy 'Learns' to Care" (Chapter 3), and "Training Starfish Babies to Play" (Chapter 4). You may also want to consider other challenging stories, such as "Clever Baby/Bad Baby" (Chapter 3) and "The Baby Fix" (Chapter 4).

Difficult and sometimes negative things challenge us. Either we can turn away and ignore them, or we can use them to help us grow by thinking more deeply about what we know and believe and what facts support our convictions. The chasm of difference between the Laboratory Greenhouse Baby Room and the others, when I experienced them, was so vast that at the time it caused me to reexamine some of my own beliefs. In the end, that reflection left me more convinced than ever that although there are shades of gray about recommended practice with infants and toddlers as I witnessed them in the other three rooms, the Laboratory Greenhouse Baby Room definitely represented a wrong way to do things. I came away from my experiences a much stronger advocate for respecting the dignity and personhood of babies, and I have become more direct and straightforward when giving students and families my recommendations for infant/toddler care and education and rationales for that advice.

The journey of writing this book allowed me to apply the perspective of time and (hopefully) some accumulated wisdom from age, distance, and time spent in further self-reflection. I hope by my sharing my stories and reflections of those experiences, readers are encouraged to imagine *what could be*, *what should not be*, and to think about how this influences their perspective on *what they do* in their own practice and programs.

A CALL TO CARE

As I come to the close of this book, I call on everyone, whether in the field of Early Childhood *Care* and Education or not, to *care for*, *about*, and

Figure 6.1. In Our Hands

with all babies and their families who spend their days in baby rooms. I call on current and future care teachers to be compassionate and sensitive in your responses to babies, treating them with the respect they deserve as fellow human beings. I call on administrators of ECCE programs to consciously and mindfully address issues that impact the well-being of the care teachers and other adults in your setting—including yourselves. I call upon researchers to devote more time and effort to examining what happens in baby rooms and deliberating on why it is important. I call on policymakers who interpret the research to implement caring policies that support a holistic view of well-being in your childcare programs, schools, and communities. I call on teacher educators of pre- and inservice ECCE professionals to guide them toward an understanding of well-being, for themselves and the children and families in their work and personal lives. And finally, I call on all of us, as global citizens, to care together for the todays and the tomorrows of all of our babies and young children, their families, and their care teachers.

References

Ackerman, D. J. (2006). The costs of being a child care teacher: Revisiting the problem of low wages. *Educational Policy, 20*, 85–112.

Ackerman, D. J. (2008). Continuity of care, professional community, and the policy context. Potential benefits for infant and toddler teachers' professional development. *Early Education and Development, 19*, 753–772.

Adamson, L. B. (2018). *Communication development during infancy.* Routledge.

Aguillard, A. E., Pierce, S. H., Benedict, J. H., & Burts, D. C. (2005). Barriers to the implementation of continuity of care practices in child care centers. *Early Childhood Research Quarterly, 20*, 329–344.

Allard, L. T., & Hunter, A. (n.d.). *Understanding temperament in infants and toddlers.* Center on the Social and Emotional Foundations for Early Learning. http://csefel.vanderbilt.edu/resources/wwb/wwb23.html

American Journal of Play. (2009). The importance of fantasy, fairness, and friendship in children's play: An interview with Vivian Gussin Paley. *American Journal of Play, 2*(2) 121–138.

Anderson, L. S. (2018). Building empathy, strengthening relationships: The benefits of multiage classrooms for young children and their caregivers. *Young Children, 73*(3), 34–42.

Austin, L. J. E. (2018). *Supporting the infant-toddler workforce: A multi-pronged approach is urgently needed.* Center for the Study of Child Care Employment. https://cscce.berkeley.edu/supporting-the-infant-toddler-workforce/

Balaban, N. (2006). Easing the separation process for infants, toddlers, and families. *Beyond the Journal: Young Children on the Web.* https://childhealthand development.files.wordpress.com/2011/06/primary-caregiving.pdf

Bandura, A. (1977). *Social learning theory.* Prentice Hall.

Basye, D. (2018, July 6). The power of autonomy: Agentic learning in the classroom. *Education and Technology Blog.* https://www.clarity-innovations.com/blog/dbasye/power-autonomy-agentic-learning-classroom

Ben-Arieh, A., Casas, F., Frones, I., & Korbin, J. E. (2014). Multifaceted concept of child well-being. In A. Ben-Arieh, F. Casas, I. Frones, & J. E. Korbin (Eds.), *Handbook of child well-being: Theories, methods and policies in global perspective* (pp. 1–27). Springer.

Bergen, D., Reid, R., & Torelli, L. (2008). *Educating and caring for very young children: The infant/toddler curriculum* (2nd ed.). Teachers College Press.

Berk, L. (2019). *Exploring child development.* Pearson Education.

Bernhardt, J. L. (2000). A primary caregiving system for infants and toddlers: Best for everyone involved. *Young Children, 55*(2), 74–80.

Biesta, G., Priestley, M., & Robinson, S. (2015). Teachers' professional agency in contradictory times. *Teachers and Teaching, 21,* 624–640.

Bjørnestad, E., Broekhuizen, M., Os, E., & Baustad, A. (2020). Interaction quality in Norwegian ECEC for toddlers measured with the Caregiver Interaction Profile (CIP) scales. *Scandinavian Journal of Educational Research, 64,* 901–920.

Bodrova, E., & Leong, D. J. (2007). *Tools of the mind: The Vygotskian approach to early childhood education* (2nd ed.). Pearson Education.

Boris, V. (2017, December 20). What makes storytelling so effective for learning? *Leading the Way* (Harvard Business Publishing). https://www.harvardbusiness.org/what-makes-storytelling-so-effective-for-learning/

Boukydis, C. Z., & Burgess, R. L. (1982). Adult physiological response to infant cries: Effects of temperament of infant, parental status, and gender. *Child Development, 53,* 1291–1298.

Bowlby, R. (2007). Babies and toddlers in non-parental daycare can avoid stress and anxiety if they develop a lasting secondary attachment bond with one carer who is consistently accessible to them. *Attachment & Human Development, 9,* 307–319.

Bratsch-Hines, M. E., Carr, R., Zgourou, E., Vernon-Feagans, L., & Willoughby, M. (2020). Infant and toddler child-care quality and stability in relation to proximal and distal academic and social outcomes. *Child Development, 91,* 1854–1864.

Breault, R. A. (2009). Distilling wisdom from practice: Finding meaning in PDS stories. *Teaching and Teacher Education, 26,* 399–407.

Brennan, M. (2014). *Perezhivanie:* What have we missed about infant care? *Contemporary Issues in Early Childhood, 15*(3), 284–292. https://doi.org/10.2304/ciec.2014.15.3.284

Bruner, E. M. (1984). Introduction: The opening up of anthropology. In S. Plattner & E. M. Bruner (Eds.), *Text, play, and story: The construction and reconstruction of self and society—1983 proceedings of the American ethnological society* (pp. 1–16). American Ethnological Society.

Burchinal, M. (2018). Measuring early care and education quality. *Child Development Perspectives, 12,* 3–9.

Business Research Company. (2019). *Child care market.* Business Research Company. https://www.thebusinessresearchcompany.com/report/child-care-market

Bussey, K., & Hill, D. (2017). Care as curriculum: Investigating teachers' views on the learning in care. *Early Child Development and Care, 187,* 128–137.

Bust, E., & Pedro, A. (2020) 'Your baby's life depends on those first 1000 days': Community health workers' perspectives of the first 1000 days of life. *Early Child Development and Care.* https://doi.org/10.1080/03004430.2020.1815720

Cárcamo, R. A., Vermeer, H. J., van der Veer, R., & van IJzendoorn, M. H. (2016). Early full-time day care, mother-child attachment, and quality of the home environment in Chile: Preliminary findings. *Early Education and Development, 27*(4), 457–477. https://doi.org/10.1080/10409289.2016.1091971

Carter, K. (1993). The place of story in the study of teaching and teacher education. *Educational Researcher, 22,* 5–12, 18. https://doi.org/10.2307/1177300

Cassidy, D., Hestenes, L., Hansen, J., Hedge, A., Shim, J., & Hestenes, S. (2005). Revisiting the two faces of child care quality: Structure and process. *Early Education and Development, 16*, 505–520.

Center for Parenting Education. (n.d.). *Understanding goodness of fit.* https://centerforparentingeducation.org/library-of-articles/child-development/understanding-goodness-of-fit/

Cherrstrom, C. A., & Boden, C. J. (2020). Expanding role and potential of curation in education: A systematic review of the literature. *The Reference Librarian, 61*(2), 113–132. https://doi.org/10.1080/02763877.2020.1776191

Cherry, K. (2021). *How observational learning affects behavior.* Very Well Mind. https://www.verywellmind.com/what-is-observational-learning-2795402

Chess, S., Thomas, A., Rutter, M., & Birch, H. G. (1963). Interaction of temperament and environment in the production of behavioral disturbances in children. *American Journal of Psychiatry, 120*, 142–148.

Clandinin, D. J., & Rosiek, J. (2007). Mapping a landscape of narrative inquiry: Borderland spaces and tensions. In D. J. Clandinin (Ed.), *Handbook of narrative inquiry: Mapping a methodology* (pp. 35–75). Sage.

Clarà, M. (2016). Vygotsky and Vasilyuk on *perezhivanie*: Two notions and one word. *Mind, Culture, and Activity, 23*(4), 284–293. https://doi.org/10.1080/10749039.2016.1186194

CLASP (Center for Law and Social Policy). (2015). *Charting progress for babies in childcare.* https://www.clasp.org/babiesinchildcare/recommendations

Cooper, M., Siu, C. T., McMullen, M. B., Rockel, J., & Powell, S. (2022). A multi-layered dialogue: Exploring Froebel's influence on pedagogies of care with one-year-olds across four cultures. *Global Education Review 10*(1).

Costa, M., & McMullen, M. B. (2020). Deliberating on the cultural meanings of teachers' practices in the care of 1-year-olds in the United States and Hong Kong. *Journal of Research in Childhood Education, 35*(4), 666–686. https://doi.org/10.1080/02568543.2020.1821136

Cryer, D., Hurwitz, S., & Wolery, M. (2000). Continuity of caregiver for infants and toddlers in center-based child care: Report on a survey of center practices. *Early Childhood Research Quarterly, 15*, 497–514.

Cryer, D., Wagner-Moore, L., Burchinal, M., Yazejian, N., Hurwitz, S., & Wolery, M. (2005). Effects of transitions to new child care classes on infant/toddler distress and behavior. *Early Childhood Research Quarterly, 20*, 37–56.

Csikszentmihalyi, M. (2008). *Flow: The psychology of optimal experience.* Harper Perennial Modern Classics. (Original work published 1991)

Cumming, T. (2017). Early childhood educators' well-being: An updated review of the literature. *Early Childhood Education Journal, 45*, 583–593.

Cumming, T., & Wong, S. (2018). Towards a holistic conceptualization of early childhood educators' work-related well-being. *Contemporary Issues in Early Childhood, 20*, 265–281.

Cummings, E. E. (2016). *E. E. Cummings complete poems, 1904–1962.* Liveright.

Cusick, S., & Georgieff, M. K. (2013, April 12). *The first 1,000 days of life: The brain's window of opportunity.* UNICEF. https://www.unicef-irc.org/article/958-the-first-1000-days-of-life-the-brains-window-of-opportunity.html

Dalgaard, N. T., Bondebjerg, A., Klokker, R., Viinholt, B. C. A., & Dietrichson, J. (2020). Protocol: Adult/child ratio and group size in early childhood education or care to promote the development of children aged 0–5 years: A systematic review. *Campbell Systematic Reviews, 16*. https://doi.org/10.1002/cl2.1079

Dalli, C., White, E., Rockel, J., & Duhn, I. (2011). *Quality early childhood education for under-two-year-olds: What should it look like? A literature review.* Ministry of Education, New Zealand. https://thehub.swa.govt.nz/assets/documents/41442_QualityECE_Web-22032011_0.pdf

Davidov, M., Zahn-Waxler, C., Roth-Hanania, R., & Knafo, A. (2013). Concern for others in the first year of life: Theory, evidence, and avenues for research. *Child Development Perspectives, 7*(2), 126–131.

Day, C. (2018). Professional identity matters: Agency, emotions, and resilience. In P. A. Schutz, J. Hong, & D. Cross Francis (Eds.), *Research on teacher identity* (pp. 61–70). Springer.

DeAngelis, T. (2008). The two faces of oxytocin: Why does the "tend and befriend" hormone come into play at the best and worst of times? *Science Watch, 39*(2).

Dennis, S. E., & O'Connor, E. (2013). Reexamining quality in early childhood education: Exploring the relationship between the organizational climate and the classroom. *Journal of Research in Childhood Education, 27*, 74–92.

Derman-Sparks, L., & Edwards, J. O. (2020). *Anti-bias education for young children and ourselves* (2nd ed.). NAEYC.

de Schipper, J. C., van IJzendoorn, M. H., & Tavecchio, L. W. C. (2004). Stability in center day care: Relations with children's well-being and problem behavior in day care. *Social Development, 13*(4), 531–550. https://doi.org/10.1111/j.1467-9507.2004.00282.x

Diebold, T., & Perren, S. (2019). The impact of childcare-group situational age. *European Journal of Developmental Psychology, 7*, 598–615.

Doucet, F. (2019). Culturally sustaining and humanizing practice in early childhood care and education. In C. P. Brown, M. B. McMullen, & N. File (Eds.). *The Wiley handbook of early childhood care and education* (pp. 149–172). John Wiley & Sons.

Douglass, A. (2011). Improving family engagement: The organizational context and its influence on partnering with parents in formal child care settings. *Early Childhood Research and Practice, 13*(2). https://ecrp.illinois.edu/v13n2/douglass.html

Douglass, A. (2016). Resilience in change: Positive perspectives on the dynamics of change in early childhood systems. *Journal of Early Childhood Research, 14*, 211–225.

Douglass, A. (2018). Positive relationships at work in early childhood education. In M. A. Warren & S. I. Donaldson (Eds.), *Toward a positive psychology of relationships: New directions in theory and research* (pp. 93–117). Praeger/ABC-CLIO.

Drugli, M. B., & Undheim, A. M. (2011). Relationships between young children in full-time day care and their caregivers: A qualitative study of parental and caregiver perspectives. *Early Child Development and Care, 182*, 1155–1165.

Dunst, C. J., & Kassow, D. Z. (2008). Caregiver sensitivity, contingent social responsiveness, and secure infant attachment. *Journal of Early and Intensive Behavior Intervention, 5*(1), 40–56.

Dunst, C. J., Espe-Sherwindt, M., & Hamby, D. W. (2019). Does capacity-building professional development engender practitioners' use of capacity-building family-centered practices? *European Journal of Educational Research, 8*(2), 515–526.

Ebbeck, M., Phoon, D. M., Tan-Chong, E. C., Tan, M. A., & Goh, M. L. (2015). A research study on secure attachment using the primary caregiving approach. *Early Childhood Education Journal, 43*(3), 233–240.

Edwards, C. P., Gandini, L., & Forman, G. (Eds.). (2011). *The hundred languages of children: The Reggio Emilia experience in transformation* (3rd ed.). Praeger.

Eisenberg, N. (1992). *The caring child.* Harvard University Press.

Eisenberg, N., Fabes, R. A., & Spinrad, T. L. (2006). Prosocial development. In W. Damon & R. M. Lerner (Series Eds.) & N. Eisenberg (Vol. Ed.), *Handbook of child psychology (Vol. 3): Social, emotional, and personality development* (6th ed., pp. 646–718). John Wiley & Sons.

Eisenberg, N., Spinrad, T. L., & Knafo-Noam, A. (2015). Prosocial development. In M. E. Lamb & R. M. Lerner (Eds.), *Handbook of child psychology and developmental science: Socioemotional processes* (pp. 610–656). John Wiley & Sons.

Elfer, P., (2013). *Key persons in the nursery: Building relationships for quality provision.* Routledge.

Elicker, J., Ruprecht, K. M., & Anderson, T. (2014). Observing infants' and toddlers' relationships and interactions in group care. In L. J. Harrison & J. Sumsion (Eds.), *Lived spaces of infant-toddler education and care: Exploring diverse perspectives on theory, research, and practice* (pp. 131–145). Springer.

Emirbayer, M., & Mische, A. (1998). What is agency? *American Journal of Sociology, 103,* 962–1023.

Ereky-Stevens, K., Funder, A., Katschnig, T., Malmbert, L., & Datler, W. (2018). Relationship building between toddlers and new caregivers in out-of-home childcare: Attachment security and caregiver sensitivity. *Early Childhood Research Quarterly, 42,* 270–279.

Eriksson, C. (2018). The art of displacement—curating a preschool context in a public transport system. *Children's Geographies, 18,* 450–462. https://doi.org/10.1080/14733285.2019.1668913

Fagard, J., Rat-Fisher, L., Esseily, R., Somogyi, E., & O'Regan, J. K. (2016). What does it take for an infant to learn how to use a tool by observation? *Frontiers in Psychology.* https://doi.org/10.3389/fpsyg.2016.00267

Fleer, M., González Rey, F., & Veresov, N. (Eds.). (2017). *Perezhivanie, emotions and subjectivity: Advancing Vygotsky's legacy.* Springer.

Garrity, S., Longstreth, S., & Atwashmi, M. (2015). A qualitative examination of the implementation of continuity of care: An organizational learning perspective. *Early Childhood Research Quarterly, 36,* 64–78.

Gartrell, D. (2012). *Education for a civil society: How guidance teaches young children democratic life skills.* NAEYC.

Geangu, E., Benga, O., Stahl, D., & Striano, T. (2010). Contagious crying beyond the first days of life. *Infant Behavior and Development, 33*(3), 279–288.

Gerber, M., & Johnson, A. (2002). *Your self-confident baby. How to encourage your child's natural abilities from the start.* John Wiley & Sons.

Gillespie, L. G., & Greenberg, J. D. (2017). Empowering infants' and toddlers' learning through scaffolding. *Young Children, 72*(2), 90–93.

Gilliam, W. S., Maupin, A. N., Reyes, C. R., Accavitti, M., & Shic, F. (2016). *Do early educators' implicit biases regarding sex and race relate to behavior expectations and recommendations of preschool expulsions and suspensions?* Yale University Child Study Center. https://medicine.yale.edu/childstudy/zigler /publications/Preschool%20Implicit%20Bias%20Policy%20Brief_final_9 _26_276766_5379_v1.pdf

Goldstein, A., Hamm, K., & Schumacher, R. (2007). *Supporting growth and development of babies in child care: What does the research say?* CLASP; Zero to Three. https://www.zerotothree.org/resources/208-supporting-growth -and-development-of-babies-in-child-care-what-does-the-research-say

Gonzalez-Mena, J. (2012). *Child, family, and community: Family-centered early care and education* (6th ed.). Pearson.

Goodwin, A. L., Cheruvu, R., & Genishi, C. (2008). Responding to multiple diversities in early childhood education. In C. Genishi, & A. L. Goodwin (Eds.), *Diversities in early childhood education: Rethinking and doing* (pp. 3–10). Routledge.

Goouch, K., & Powell, S. (2013). *The baby room.* Open University Press.

Hamlin, J. K., (2013). Moral judgment and action in preverbal infants and toddlers: Evidence for an innate moral core. *Current Directions in Psychological Science, 22*(3), 186–193.

Hammond, R. A. (2009). *Respecting babies: A new look at Magda Gerber's RIE approach.* Zero to Three.

Hanh, T. N. (1999). *The miracle of mindfulness: A manual on meditation.* Beacon Press.

Hart, C. S., & Brando, N. (2018). A capability approach to children's well-being, agency and participatory rights in education. *European Journal of Education, Research, Development and Policy, 53*(3), 293–305.

Head Start/ECLKC. (2020). *Promoting staff well-being.* U.S. Department of Health and Human Services. https://eclkc.ohs.acf.hhs.gov/mental-health /article/promoting-staff-well-being

Hegde, A. V., & Cassidy, D. J. (2004). Teacher and parent perspectives on looping. *Early Childhood Education Journal, 32*, 133–138.

Honig, A. S. (2002). *Secure relationships: Nurturing infant/toddler attachment in early care settings.* NAEYC.

Horm, D. M., File, N., Bryant, D., Burchinal, M., Raikes, H., Forestieri, N., Encinger, A., & Cobo-Lewis, A. (2018). Associations between continuity of care in infant-toddler classrooms and child outcomes. *Early Childhood Research Quarterly, 42*, 105–118.

Horm, D. M., Goble, C. B., & Branscomb, K. R. (2012). Infant toddler curriculum: Review, reflection, and revolution. In N. File, J. J. Mueller, & D. B. Wisneski (Eds.), *Curriculum in early childhood education: Re-examined, rediscovered, renewed* (pp. 105–119). Taylor & Francis.

Institute of Medicine and National Research Council. (2012). *From neurons to neighborhoods: An update: Workshop summary.* The National Academies Press. https://doi.org/10.17226/13119

Jančec, L., Vorkapić, S. T., & Vodopivec, J. L. (2019). Hidden curriculum determinants in (pre)school institutions: Implicit cognition in action. In Information Resources Management Association (Ed.), *Early childhood development: Concepts, methodologies, tools, and applications* (Vol. 1, pp. 101–128). IGI Global.

Jeon, L., Buettner, C. K., & Grant, A. A. (2018). Early childhood teachers' psychological well-being: Exploring potential predictors of depression, stress, and emotional exhaustion. *Early Education and Development, 29*(1). https://doi.org/10.1080/10409289.2017.1341806

Jin, K. S., Houston, J. L., Baillargeon, R., Grohd, A. M., & Roisman, G. I. (2018). Young infants expect an unfamiliar adult to comfort a crying baby: Evidence from a standard violation-of-expectation task and a novel infant-triggered-video task. *Cognitive Psychology, 102*, 1–20.

Jung, J., & Recchia, S. (2013). Scaffolding infants' play through empowering and individualizing teaching practices. *Early Education and Development, 24*, 829–850.

Katsiada, E., Roufidou, I., Wainwright, J., & Angeli, V. (2018). Young children's agency: Exploring children's interactions with practitioners and ancillary staff members in Greek early childhood education and care settings. *Early Child Development and Care, 188*, 937–950.

Keating, K., Daily, S., Cole, P., Murphey, D., Pina, G., Ryberg, R., Moron, L., & Laurore, J. (2019). *State of babies yearbook: 2019.* Zero to Three and Child Trends. https://stateofbabies.org/wp-content/uploads/2019/02/State-of-Babies-Yearbook_national-profile_2.25.19.pdf

Keyser, J. (20017). *From parents to partners: Building a family-centered early childhood program* (2nd ed.). Redleaf Press.

Kim, Y. (2016). Relationship-based developmentally supportive approach to infant childcare practice. *Early Childhood Development and Care, 186*, 734–749.

Knafo, A., Zahn-Waxler, C., Van Hulle, C., Robinson, S. H., & Rhee, S. H. (2008). The developmental origins of a disposition toward empathy: Genetic and environmental contributions. *Emotion, 8*, 737–752.

Köster, M., Ohmer, X., Nguyen, T. D., & Kärtner, J. (2016). Infants understand others' needs. *Psychological Science, 27*(4), 542–548. https://doi.org/10.1177/0956797615627426

Kramer, S. (1946). "There was a little girl": Its first printings: Its authorship: Its variants. *The Papers of the Bibliographical Society of America, 40*(4), 287–310.

Kurcinka, M. S. (2006). *Raising your spirited child: A guide for parents whose child is more intense, sensitive, perceptive, persistent, and energetic.* William Morrow.

Kwon, K.-A., Ford, T., G., Jeon, L., Malek-Laseter, A., Randall, K., Ellis, N., Kile, M., & Salvatore, A. (2021). Testing a holistic conceptual framework for early childhood teacher well-being. *Journal of School Psychology, 86*, 178–197.

Kwon, K.-A, Jeon, S. Jeon, L., & Castle, S. (2019). The role of teachers' depressive symptoms in classroom quality and children's developmental outcomes in Early Head Start programs, *Learning and Individual Differences, 74*(101748). https://doi.org/10.1016/j.lindif.2019.06.002

Kwon, K.-A., Malek, A., Horm, D., & Castle, S. (2020). Turnover and retention of infant-toddler teachers: Reasons, consequences, and implications for practice and policy. *Children and Youth Services Review, 115*(105061). https://doi .org/10.1016/j.childyouth.2020.105061

Lally, J. R. (Ed.). (2011). *A guide to social-emotional growth and socialization* (2nd ed.). California Department of Education. https://www.cde.ca.gov/sp /cd/re/documents/pitcguidesocemo2011.pdf

Lally, J. R., & Mangione, P. L. (2008). The program for infant toddler care. In J. P. Roopnarine & J. E. Johnson (Eds.), *Approaches to early childhood education* (5th ed., pp. 25–47). Prentice Hall.

Lansdown, G. (2001). *Promoting children's participation in democratic decision-making.* UNICEF. https://www.unicef-irc.org/publications/pdf/insight6.pdf

Lansdown, G. (2011). *Every child's right to be heard: A resource guide on the UN committee on the rights of the child, general comment no. 12.* Save the Children. https://studylib.net/doc/18389861/every-child-s-right-to-be-heard

Laurin, J. C., Geoffroy, M. C., Boivin, M., Japel, C., Raynault, M. F., Tremblay, R. E., & Côté, S. M. (2015). Child care services, socioeconomic inequalities, and academic performance. *Pediatrics, 136*, 1112–1124.

Lawrence-Lightfoot, S. (2005). Reflections on portraiture: A dialogue between art and science. *Qualitative Inquiry, 11*, 3–15.

Lawrence-Lightfoot, S., & Davis, J. H. (1997). *The art and science of portraiture.* Jossey-Bass.

Leavitt, R. L. (1994). *Power and emotion in infant-toddler day care.* SUNY Press.

Lerner, C., & Parlakian, R. (n.d.). *How to help your child develop empathy.* Zero to Three. https://www.zerotothree.org/resources/5-how-to-help-your-child -develop-empathy

Liddle, M. J. E., Bradley, B. S., & McGrath, A. (2015). Baby empathy: Infant distress and peer social response. *Infant Mental Health Journal, 36*, 446–458.

Lipscomb, S. T., Chandler, K. D., Abshire, C., Jaramillo, J., & Kothari, B. (2021). Early childhood teachers' self-efficacy and professional support predict work engagement. *Early Childhood Education Journal.* https://doi.org/10.1007 /s10643-021-01182-5

Loeb, S., Fuller, B., Kagan, S. L., & Carrol, B. (2004). Child care in poor communities: Early learning effects of type, quality, and stability. *Child Development, 75*(1), 47–66.

Malaguzzi, L. (n.d.). *The hundred languages. Reggio Emilia.* https://reggioemilia 2015.weebly.com/the-100-languages.html

Macmillan Dictionary. (n.d.). Curate: Definitions and synonyms. In *Macmillan Dictionary.* Retrieved December 19, 2021, from: https://www.macmilland ictionary.com/us/dictionary/american/curate_2

Mandela, N. (1995, May 8). Address by President Nelson Mandela at the launch of the Nelson Mandela Children's Fund, Pretoria. *Nelson Rolihlahla Mandela, 18 July 1918–5 December 2013.* http://www.mandela.gov.za/mandela _speeches/1995/950508_nmcf.htm

Mann, M. B., & Carney, R. N. (2008). Building positive relationships in the lives of infants and toddlers in child care. In M. R. Jalongo (Ed.), *Enduring bonds: The significance of interpersonal relationships in young children's lives* (pp. 147–157). Springer.

Maslow, A. H. (1943). A theory of human motivation. *Psychological Review, 50,* 370–396.

Matthews, G. (1998). *The philosophy of childhood.* Harvard University Press.

McCartney, K., Dearing, E., Taylor, B. A., & Bub, K. L. (2007). Quality child care supports the achievement of low-income children: Direct and indirect pathways through caregiving and the home environment. *Journal of Applied Developmental Psychology, 28,* 411–426.

McCormick, K. I., & McMullen, M. B. (2019). A North American perspective on understanding and nurturing professional well-being in the early childhood workplace. In L. Gibbs & M. Gasper (Eds.), *Challenging the intersection of policy with pedagogy* (pp. 69–84). Routledge.

McCormick, K. I., McMullen, M. B., & Lee, M. S. C. (2021). Early childhood professional well-being as a predictor of the risk of turnover in Early Head Start and Head Start settings. *Early Education and Development.* https://doi .org/10.1080/10409289.2021.1909915

McDonald, P., Thorpe, K., & Irvine, S. (2018). Low pay but still we stay: Retention in early childhood education and care. *Journal of Industrial Relations, 60*(5), 647–668. https://doi.org/10.1177/0022185618800351

McGinty, A. S., Justice, L., & Rimm-Kaufman, S. R. (2008). Sense of school community for preschool teachers serving at-risk children. *Early Education and Development, 19,* 361–384.

McMullen, M. B. (2010). Confronting the baby blues: A social constructivist reflects on time spent in a behaviorist infant classroom. *Early Childhood Research & Practice, 12*(1). https://files.eric.ed.gov/fulltext/EJ889721.pdf

McMullen, M. B. (2013). Understanding development of infants and toddlers. In C. Copple, S. Bredekamp, D. Koraleck, & K. Charner (Eds.), *Developmentally appropriate practice: Focus on infants and toddlers* (pp. 23–50). NAEYC.

McMullen, M. B. (2017). Continuity of care with infants & toddlers: Identifying benefits and addressing common concerns. *Child Care Exchange, 39*(1), 46–50.

McMullen, M. B. (2018). The multiple benefits of continuity of care for infants and toddlers, families, and caregiving staff. *Young Children, 73*(3), 38–42.

McMullen, M. B., Addleman, J., Fulford, A. M., Mooney, S., Moore, S., Sisk, S., & Zachariah, J. (2009). Learning to be me while coming to understand we: Encouraging prosocial babies in group settings. *Young Children, 64*(4), 20–28.

McMullen, M. B., & Apple, P. (2012). When babies (and their families!) are on board: Key features in the administration of relationship-based infant toddler programs. *Young Children, 16*(4), 42–48.

McMullen, M. B., & Brody, D. (2021). *The right stuff: Play materials for infants, toddlers, and twos.* NAEYC.

McMullen, M. B., Buzzelli, C., & Yun, N. R. (2016). Pedagogies of care for well-being. In T. David, S. Powell, & K. Goouch (Eds.), *Routledge international handbook of philosophies and theories of early childhood education* (pp. 259–268). Taylor & Francis.

McMullen, M. B., & Dixon, S. (2009). In support of a relationship-based approach to practice with infants and toddlers in the United States. In J. Brownlee (Ed.), *Participatory learning and the early years* (pp. 109–128). Routledge.

McMullen, M. B., & Lash, M. (2012). Babies on campus: Considering service to infants and families among other competing forces in university-affiliated programs. *Early Childhood Research & Practice, 14*(2).

McMullen, M. B., Lee, M., McCormick, K. I., & Choi, J. (2020). Early childhood professional well-being as a predictor of the risk of turnover in childcare. *Journal of Research in Childhood Education, 34,* 331–335.

McMullen, M. B., & McCormick, K. I. (2016). Flourishing in transactional care systems: Caring with infant and toddler caregivers about wellbeing. In D. Navaez, J. Braungart-Rieker, L. Miller, L. Gettler, & P. Hastings (Eds.), *Contexts for young child flourishing: Evolution, family, and society* (pp. 267–287). Oxford University Press.

McMullen, M. B., McCormick, K. I., & Lee, M. (2018). Caring for the well-being of early childhood care and education professionals. *Child Care Exchange, 42*(1), 16–19.

McMullen, M. B., Yun, N., Mihai, A., & Kim, H. J. (2015). Experiences of parents and professionals in well-established continuity of care infant toddler programs. *Early Education and Development, 27*(2), 190–220. https://doi .org/10.1080/10409289.2016.1102016

Munday, A. (2018). What is autonomy in early childhood education? *Early Childhood Education Blog.* https://www.himama.com/blog/what-is-autonomy -in-early-childhood-education/

National Institutes of Health. (2013). *Women's, men's brains respond differently to hungry infant's cries: NIH study documents gender variations in brain activity.* https://www.nih.gov/news-events/news-releases/womens-mens-brains -respond-differently-hungry-infants-cries

National Resource Center for Family Centered Practice. (n.d.). *What is family centered practice?* University of Iowa. https://clas.uiowa.edu/nrcfcp/what -family-centered-practice

NICHD Early Child Care Research Network. (2002). Child-care structure → process → outcome: Direct and indirect effects of child-care quality on young children's development. *Psychological Science, 13*(3), 199–206. https://doi .org/10.1111/1467-9280.00438

Noddings, N. (1991). Stories in dialogue: Caring and interpersonal reasoning. In C. Witherell & N. Noddings (Eds.), *Stories lives tell: Narrative and dialogue in education* (pp. 157–170). Teachers College Press.

Noddings, N., & Witherell, C. (1991). Epilogue: Themes remembered and foreseen. In C. Witherell, & N. Noddings (Eds.), *Stories lives tell: Narrative and dialogue in education* (pp. 279–280). Teachers College Press.

Novoa, C. (2020). *The child care crisis disproportionately affects children with disabilities.* Center for American Progress.

O'Connor, E., & McCartney, K. (2007). Examining teacher-child relationships and achievement as part of an ecological model of development. *American Educational Research Journal, 44*(2), 340–369.

1,000 Days. (2016). *The first 1,000 days: Nourishing America's future.* https:// thousanddays.org/wp-content/uploads/1000Days-NourishingAmericasFuture -Report-FINAL-WEBVERSION-SINGLES.pdf

Opie, J. E., McIntosh, J. E., Esler, T. B., Duschinsky, R., George, C., Schore, A., Kothe, E., Tan, E. S., Greenwood, C. J., & Olsson, C. A. (2021). Early childhood attachment stability and change: A meta-analysis. *Attachment & Human Development, 23*(6), 897–930. https://doi.org/10.1080/14616734 .2020.1800769

Owen, M. T., Klausli, J. F., Mata-Otero, A., & Caughy, M. O. (2008). Relationship-focused child care practices: Quality of care and child outcomes for children in poverty. *Early Education and Development, 19,* 302–329.

Paris, C., & Lung, P. (2008). Agency and child-centered practices in novice teachers: Autonomy, efficacy, intentionality, and reflectivity. *Journal of Early Childhood Teacher Education, 29,* 253–268.

Parlakian, R. (2017). *Helping children learn right from wrong.* Zero to Three. https://www.zerotothree.org/resources/1689-helping-children-learn-right -from-wrong

Patterson, C. (2018). Constructing narrative and phenomenological meaning within one study. *Qualitative Research Journal, 18,* 223–237.

Pauker, S., Perlman, M., Prime, H., & Jenkins, J. (2018). Caregiver cognitive sensitivity: Measure development and validation in Early Childhood Education and Care (ECEC) settings. *Early Childhood Research Quarterly, 45,* 45–57.

Paulus, M. (2014). The emergence of prosocial behavior: Why do infants and toddlers help, comfort, and share? *Child Development Perspectives, 8*(2), 77–81.

Phillips, D., Mekos, D., Scarr, S., McCartney, K., & Abbott- Shim, M. (2000). Within and beyond the classroom door: Assessing quality in childcare centers. *Early Childhood Research Quarterly, 15,* 475–496.

Piaget, J., & Smith, L. (2013). *Sociological studies.* Routledge.

Pianta, R. C., Barnett, W. S., & Justice, L. M. (Eds.). (2012). *Handbook on early childhood education.* Guilford Press.

Pilarza, A. R., & Hill, H. D. (2014). Unstable and multiple child care arrangements and young children's behavior. *Early Childhood Research Quarterly, 29,* 471–483.

Pitard, J. (2019) Autoethnography as a phenomenological tool: Connecting the personal to the cultural. In P. Liamputtong (Ed.), *Handbook of research methods in health social sciences* (pp. 1829–1845). Springer.

Polkinghorne, D. E. (1988). *SUNY series in philosophy of the social sciences. Narrative knowing and the human sciences.* SUNY Press.

Quann, V., & Wien, C. A. (2006). The visible empathy of infants and toddlers. *Young Children, 61*(4), 22–29.

Qvortrup, J. (2009). Are children human beings or human becomings? A critical assessment of outcome thinking. *Rivista Internazionale Di Scienze Sociali, 117,* 631–653.

Raghavan, R., & Alexandrova, A. (2015). Toward a theory of child well-being. *Social Indicators Research, 121*(3), 887–902. https://link.springer.com/content /pdf/10.1007/s11205-014-0665-z.pdf

Raikes, H. (1996). A secure base for babies: Applying attachment theory concepts to the infant care setting. *Young Children, 51*(5), 59–67.

Raikes, H., & Edwards, C. P. (2009). *Extending the dance in infant and toddler caregiving: Enhancing attachment and relationships.* Brookes Publishing.

Ratner, C. (2001). Agency and culture. *Journal for the Theory of Social Behaviour, 30,* 413–434.

Recchia, S. L. (2012). Caregiver–child relationships as a context for continuity in child care. *Early Years, 32(2),* 143–157. https://doi.org/10.1080/09575146 .2012.693908

Recchia, S. L., & Shin, M. (2012). In and out of synch: Infant childcare teachers' adaptations to infants' developmental changes. *Early Child Development and Care, 182,* 1545–1562.

Reidt-Parker, J., & Chainski, M. J. (n.d.). *The importance of continuity of care: Policies and practices in early childhood systems and programs.* The Ounce. https://www.startearly.org/app/uploads/2020/09/PUBLICATION_NPT-Con tinuity-of-Care-Nov-2015.pdf

Renken, E. (2020). *How stories connect and persuade us: Unleashing the brain power of narrative.* https://www.npr.org/sections/health-shots/2020/04/11 /815573198/how-stories-connect-and-persuade-us-unleashing-the-brain -power-of-narrative

Rice, D., Schmit, H., & Matthews, S. (2019). *Child care and housing: Big expenses with too little help available.* Center on Budget and Policy Priorities and CLASP. https://www.cbpp.org/research/housing/child-care-and-housing -big-expenses-with-too-little-help-available

Ridgway, A., Lian, L., Quiñones, G. (2016). Transitory moments in infant/toddler play: Agentic imagination. *International Research in Early Childhood Education, 7*(2), 91–110.

RIE: Resources for Infant Educarers. (n.d.). *About RIE.* https://rie.org/about/

Roberts, A., Gallaghera, K. C., Daroa, A. M., Irukac, I. U., Sarvera, S. L. (2019). Workforce well-being: Personal and workplace contributions to early educators' depression across settings. *Journal of Applied Developmental Psychology, 61,* 4–12.

Rodrígez García, J. M. (2001). Scientia potestas est—Knowledge is power: Francis Bacon to Michel Foucault. *Neohelicon 28,* 109–121. https://doi.org/10 .1023/A:1011901104984

Rose, F. (2011). The art of immersion: Why do we tell stories? *Wired Magazine.* https://www.wired.com/2011/03/why-do-we-tell-stories/

Rosen, T. (2018). Storytelling in teacher professional development. *Learning Landscapes, 11,* 303–317.

Ruprecht, K., Elicker, J., & Choi, J. (2015). Continuity of care, caregiver-child interactions, and toddler social competence. *Early Education and Development, 27,* 221–239.

Rutanen, N., & Hännikäinen, M. (2017). Care, upbringing and teaching in horizontal transitions in toddler day-care groups. In E. J. White, & C. Dalli (Eds.), *Under-three-year-olds in policy and practice* (pp. 57–72). Springer.

Rymanowicz, K. (2015). *Monkey see, monkey do: Model behavior in early childhood.* Michigan State University Extension. https://www.canr.msu.edu/news /monkey_see_monkey_do_model_behavior_in_early_childhood

Samman, E., & Lombardi, J. (2019). *Childcare and working families: New opportunity or missing link*. UNICEF. https://www.unicef.org/sites/default/files/2019-07/UNICEF-Childcare%20-Family-Friendly-Policies-2019.pdf

Schertz, H. H., Horn, K., Lee, M., & Mitchell, S. (2017). Supporting toddlers with autism risk make social connections. *Young Exceptional Children, 20*, 16–29.

Schwarzenberg, S. J., & Georgieff, M. (n.d.). *Your Baby's First 1,000 Days: AAP policy explained*. HealthyChildren.org, American Academy of Pediatrics. https://www.healthychildren.org/English/ages-stages/baby/Pages/Babys-First-1000-Days-AAP-Policy-Explained.aspx

Seligman, M. (2011). *Flourish: A visionary new understanding of happiness and well-being*. Free Press.

Shin, M. (2010). Peeking at the relationship world of infant friends and caregivers. *Journal of Early Childhood Research 8*, 294–302.

Shirvanian, N., & Michael, T. (2017). Implementation of attachment theory into early childhood settings. *The International Education Journal: Comparative Perspectives, 16*(2), 97–115.

Singer, E., Nederend, M., Penninx, L., Tajik, M., & Boom, J. (2014). The teacher's role in supporting young children's level of play engagement. *Early Child Development and Care, 184*, 1233–1249.

Slot, P. (2018). *Structural characteristics and process quality in early childhood education and care: A literature review* (OECD Education Working Paper No. 176). OECD. https://www.oecd.org/officialdocuments/publicdisplaydocumentpdf/?cote=EDU/WKP(2018)12&docLanguage=En

Solomon, D. C. (2013). *Baby knows best: Raising a confident and resourceful child, the RIE way*. Little Brown Spark.

Sorbring, E., & Kuczynski, L. (2018). Children's agency in the family, in school and in society: Implications for health and well-being. *International Journal of Qualitative Studies on Health and Well-being, 13*(1, Supp. 1). https://doi.org/10.1080/17482631.2019.1634414

Souto-Manning, M., & Rabadi-Raol, A. (2018). (Re)centering quality in early childhood education: Toward intersectional justice for minoritized children. *Review of Research in Education, 42*(1), 203–225. https://doi.org/10.3102/0091732X18759550

Sravanti, L. (2017). Goodness of fit. *Indian Journal of Psychiatry, 59*, 515. doi: 10.4103/psychiatry.IndianJPsychiatry_423_17 Available at https://journals.lww.com/indianjpsychiatry/Fulltext/2017/59040/Goodness_of_fit.21.aspx

Sroufe, L. A. (2005). Attachment and development: A prospective, longitudinal study from birth to adulthood. *Attachment and Human Development, 7*, 349–367.

Start Early. (2020). Why intervene early. https://www.startearly.org/post/why-intervene-early/

Sutton, J. (2011). *My writing year: Making sense of being a writer*. Mad Dog Publishing.

Swap, W., Leonard, D., Shields, M., & Abrams, L. (2015). Using mentoring and storytelling to transfer knowledge in the workplace. *Journal of Management Information Systems, 1*, 95–114.

Thomas, A., Chess, S., & Birch, H. G. (1970). The origin of personality. *Scientific American, 223*(2), 102–109.

Thompson, R. (2014). Why are relationships important to children's well-being? In A. BenArieh, F. Casas, I. Frones, & J. E. Korbin (Eds.), *Handbook of child well-being: Theories, method; and policies in global perspective* (pp. 1917–1954). Springer.

Thorpe, K., Jansen, E., Sullivan, V., Irvine, S., & McDonald, P. (2020). Identifying predictors of retention and professional well-being of the early childhood education workforce in a time of change. *Journal of Educational Change, 21*, 623–647.

Trevarthen, C. (2008). The musical art of infant conversation: Narrating in the time of sympathetic experience, without rational interpretation, before words. *Musicae Scientiae, 12*, 15–46.

Trevarthen, C., & Aitken, K. J. (2001). Infant intersubjectivity: Research, theory, and clinical applications. *Journal of Child Psychology and Psychiatry, 42*, 3–48.

Trevarthen C., & Delafield-Butt J. (2017). Intersubjectivity in the imagination and feelings of the infant: Implications for education in the early years. In E. White & C. Dalli (Eds.), *Policy and pedagogy with under-three-year-olds: Cross-disciplinary insights and innovations* (pp. 17–39). Springer.

Tronick, E. (2007). *The neurobehavioral and social-emotional development of infants and children.* W. W. Norton.

UNICEF. (2017). *UNICEF's programme guidance for early childhood development.* https://www.unicef.org/sites/default/files/2018-12/UNICEF%20Programme%20Guidance%20for%20Early%20Childhood%20Development%202017.pdf

United Nations, Committee on the Rights of the Child. (2009). *Convention on the rights of the child: General comment #12.* United Nations.https://www2.ohchr.org/english/bodies/crc/docs/AdvanceVersions/CRC-C-GC-12.pdf

University of Southern California. (2017). Something universal occurs in the brain when it processes stories, regardless of language. *ScienceDaily.* www.sciencedaily.com/releases/2017/10/171005141710.htm

Valloton, C. D. (2009). Do infants influence their quality of care? Infants' communicative gestures predict caregivers' responsiveness. *Infant Behavior and Development, 32*, 351–365.

Vandell, D. L. (1996). Characteristics of infant child care: Factors contributing to positive caregiving: NICHD early childcare research network. *Early Childhood Research Quarterly, 11*(3), 269–306. https://doi.org/10.1016/S0885-2006(96)90009-5

Veziroglu-Celik, M., & Yildiz, T. (2018). Organizational climate in early childhood education. *Journal of Education and Training Studies, 6*(12), 88–96.

Vygotsky, L. S. (1978). *Mind in society: The development of higher psychological processes.* Harvard University Press.

Vygotsky, L. S. (1987). Thinking and speech. In R. W. Rieber & A. S. Carton (Eds.), *The collected works of L. S. Vygotsky: Vol. 1: Problems of general psychology* (pp. 39–285). Plenum Press. (Original work published 1934)

Waldman, D. J. (2005). *Age-by-age guide to baby friendships: How babies develop relationships with one another.* Explore Parents. https://www.parents.com/baby/development/social/age-by-age-guide-to-baby-friendships/

Wesley, P. W., & Buysse, V. (2001). Communities of practice: Expanding professional roles to promote reflection and shared inquiry. *Topics in Early Childhood Special Education, 21*(2), 114–123. https://doi.org/10.1177/027112140 102100205

White, E., Peter, M., & Redder, B. (2015). Infant and teacher dialogue in education and care: A pedagogical imperative. *Early Childhood Research Quarterly, 30*, 160–173.

Widrich, L. (2012). *The science of storytelling: Why telling a story is the most powerful way to activate our brains.* Lifehacker. https://lifehacker.com/the -science-of-storytelling-why-telling-a-story-is-the-5965703

Williams, A. (2009). On the tip of creative tongues. *New York Times.* https:// www.nytimes.com/2009/10/04/fashion/04curate.html

Williams, S. T., Mastergeorge, A. M., & Ontai, L. L. (2010). Caregiver involvement in infant peer interactions: Scaffolding in a social context. *Early Childhood Research Quarterly, 25*, 251–266.

Wittmer, D. S., & Honig, A. S. (2020). *Day to day: The relationship way.* NAEYC.

Workman, S., & Jessen-Howard, S. (2018). Understanding the true cost of child care for infants and toddlers. Center for American Progress. https://www .americanprogress.org/issues/early-childhood/reports/2018/11/15/460970 /understanding-true-cost-child-care-infants-toddlers/

Wright, B. L. (2021). What about the children? Teachers cultivating and nurturing the voice and agency of young children. *Young Children, 76*(2), 28–32.

Zak, P. J. (2013). How stories change the brain. *Greater Good Magazine.* https:// greatergood.berkeley.edu/article/item/how_stories_change_brain

Zeanah, C. H. (2019). *Handbook of infant mental health* (4th ed.). Guilford Press.

Zero to Three. (n.d.). *Tuning into temperament.* https://www.zerotothree.org /resources/series/tuning-into-temperament#the-temperament-characteristics

Zero to Three. (2008). *Caring for infants and toddlers in groups: Developmentally appropriate practice* (2nd ed.). Zero to Three.

Zero to Three. (2010). *Primary caregiving and continuity of care.* (Excerpted from R. Theilheimer (2006), *Molding to the children: Primary caregiving and continuity of care. Zero to Three, 26, 3).* https://www.zerotothree.org /resources/85-primary-caregiving-and-continuity-of-care

Zero to Three. (2016). *From cries to conversations: The development of communication skills from birth to 3. [Video].* https://www.zerotothree.org/resources /196-from-cries-to-conversations-the-development-of-communication-skills -from-birth-to-3

Zero to Three. (2017). *Infant-toddler child care fact sheet.* Zero to Three. https:// www.zerotothree.org/resources/2012-infant-toddler-child-care-fact-sheet

Ziviani, J., Feeney, R. B., & Khan, A. (2011). Early intervention services for children with physical disability: Parents' perceptions of family-centeredness and service satisfaction. *Infants and Young Children, 24*, 364–382.

Index

About the Author

Mary Benson McMullen, PhD, is a professor of early childhood education at Indiana University (IU), where she has been on the faculty since 1993. She received a BS from Michigan State University and earned MS and PhD degrees in child development from Florida State University. During and after her graduate education, she worked as a care teacher of infants, toddlers, and preschoolers and then as an early childhood program director, before accepting her faculty position. Mary, who is the recipient of numerous teaching and mentoring awards, teaches courses at IU to preservice and inservice early childhood care and education professionals, as well as to doctoral students who plan to become early childhood teacher educators and research scholars. Mary's primary research interests involve factors that influence quality early care and education for infants and toddlers; the healthy overall growth, development, learning, and well-being of young children (birth through age 5); how "pedagogies of care" are reflected in the beliefs and practices of teaching and care professionals across cultures and contexts; and factors that influence and ensure the well-being of the adults who work with young children and families in various capacities. She has published more than 50 articles for research and teaching journals as well as over a dozen book chapters; and she is coauthor with Dylan Brody of *Infants and Toddlers at Play: Choosing the Right Stuff for Learning & Development* (NAEYC, 2021) and coeditor with Christopher Brown and Nancy File of *The Wiley Handbook of Early Childhood Care and Education* (Wiley/Blackwell, 2019). Mary lives in Bloomington, Indiana, where she and her husband of 40 years raised their three sons.

Printed and bound by CPI Group (UK) Ltd, Croydon, CR0 4YY

09/06/2025

14685976-0002